TRANSFORMING THE QUEEN

A Woman's Story of Personal Repentance

by Diane Ehrlich

Reform Ministry Publications

Transforming The Queen
A Woman's Story of Personal Repentance

Published by: Reform Ministry Publications
Cleveland, Ohio
www.reformministry.com

ISBN: 1453828575
ISBN-13: 9781453828571

"'I will bring him near and he will come close to me, for who is he who will devote himself to be close to me?' declares the Lord."

Jeremiah 30:21 NIV

CONTENTS

ACKNOWLEDGMENTS

It was never my intention to study evil. All I was trying to do was understand what I was seeing. I could close my eyes and say, "Surely I am imagining this!" But I wasn't. Looking for explanations, I browsed the Christian bookstores and found many worthy topics on inner healing and spiritual warfare, but I found non that categorized sin in the way that I was seeing.

As a result, I continually questioned God and He answered me with verses that explained about human nature. I learned that, for the unbeliever, sin is tolerable though annoying. It provokes questions, but in it there are no solutions. Sin is crippling and yet, as long as he can keep going, the sinner thinks he is fine.

But for the Christian, evil seen under the guidance of Truth is unbearable. It is hell exposed but not experienced for eternity. A strong dose of it should send us running to Christ, grateful for His merciful provision.

This leads me to say that I was only able to write at length about sin because God enabled me. He gave me the power to inspect it, describe it, and then turn and flee from it. Sometimes I thought I couldn't stand any more, but He always came with complete relief.

In giving all credit to God, I also credit Him for providing special friends who expressed His care. I greatly appreciate the help of everyone who read and gave suggestions at different stages of this writing. They are K. Marie David, Dawn McNamee and Kevin Taylor. Special thanks to Bible teacher and friend James P. Clevenger for consulting with me on doctrine and format. I also want to mention Dan Chapin for computer consulting and Jill Riegel for artwork.

I am grateful to those who were supportive and encouraged me to complete this project. Those people are my parents, Harold and Melba Ehrlich, my pastor Rev. Herbert Smith and my church family at Sanctuary Baptist Church.

Although there is considerable time spent alone writing, I thank God for rich moments together as He whispered His secrets in my ear.

INTRODUCTION

Iam basically a morning person. Like a quarterback at the hike, I am ready to carry out the day's business at work by 8:01 a.m. Even more, I am a happy, humming, singing, smiling morning person. Though my intentions are good, I have to check the tolerance level of my co-workers who groan and slowly move away, hugging their favorite mug of soothing morning coffee.

King Solomon was wise to morning people when he wrote, **"If a man loudly blesses his neighbor in the morning, it will be taken as a curse." (Proverbs 27:14 NIV)** My conscience reminds me that a tad too much vivacity in the early hours would be a shock to the system of some unsuspecting non-morning person. But to hold back the surge of morning energy would be like trying to stop Niagara Falls from falling—the river of joy inside of me must flow! Morning is a delight to me today, and I can only credit my happiness to the new life God has given me through Jesus Christ.

To know me now, no one would guess that I haven't always been this cheerful. Few remember how I spent years trying to make life work and failed miserably. Eventually, I became so deeply depressed that I didn't have enough "umph" to get out of bed in the morning to go to work.

Only God could see the countless changes that would be necessary to make such a dramatic difference. He was the One who came with power to change me. This verse describes exactly what He did: **"He lifted me out of the slimy pit, out of the mud and mire; he set my feet on a rock and gave me a firm place to**

stand. He put a new song in my mouth, a hymn of praise to our God." (Psalm 40: 2 NIV)

One would think that it would be easy to detect being stuck in a slimy pit, helplessly sinking in the mud. Although this was my condition, I didn't know it. Nor did I realize the complexity of my personal sin that was weighing me down in the muck. I had to be shown from Christ's point of view how I was living and why life wasn't working.

This, then, is my story of how I came to understand the seriousness of my sin and how God was able to remedy my spiritual illness. As I learned to cooperate with Christ, God cleared away the unclean thoughts and emotions that clogged my heart and set me free to sing a song of real happiness.

PART I

AUDIENCE WITH THE QUEEN

∾ Chapter 1 ∾
I DID IT MY WAY

LITTLE MISS POPULARITY

Much of my trouble began in high school when I thought that popularity meant happiness. I would stare at the cheerleaders in front of the crowds at the games and say to myself, "I want what they have!" This idea made me spend hours at home in front of our side door window practicing jumps. After much work, my wish came true and I made the team in the twelfth grade.

Truthfully though, I didn't understand enough about football to even like it. I had secretly hoped that the status of being a cheerleader would cure me of my teenage insecurities. I thought the weekend limelight would surely mask the weekday uneasiness of being shy and self-conscious. Whatever faking I had to do to be liked would be well worth it to make my senior year bearable.

Maybe then I wouldn't feel so lonely without my boyfriend. For two years I had been caught up in a steady relationship with an upperclassman, and now he was away at college. My involvement with him had left little time for other friends. Now, as a senior, I was desperately alone.

The relationship wasn't especially good, but the romance kept me attached.

"I love you and I want to marry you!" he told me through tears. When the scene was over, I decided to give him one more try. I had broken up with him a number of times before because I felt he was

3

telling me lies. He always offered excuses and then told me I was the only one he could ever love. I was sick of believing. I didn't know what to believe anymore. But a part of me still hoped that he was the one for me. I didn't want to take a chance on losing him for good, so I promised to wait for him as he drove out of my driveway and on to college the next day.

To fill the lonely hours, I spent my time learning to sew. I cleared a space in our attic and set up a card table for my grandmother's old Singer sewing machine. There I drifted into a forgetful world of patterns, fabrics, and fashion possibilities. Fortunately, my new love was in place when the phone call came.

"Hi, this is Sandy." She was my arch-rival for my boyfriend's attentions and had been the topic of many of our arguments. I had to control my rising jealousy as she spoke.

"I think we have something important to talk about." She had my rigid attention. "You're still going steady with him, aren't you?"

"Yes," I managed, "but he asked me to keep it a secret."

"I thought so," she said. "I'm going steady with him, too!"

Her words landed with a thud. How was that possible? She and I were on the same cheerleading squad! How could he go steady with both of us at the same time?

My stomach knotted up as we went over all the details of the lie. I appreciated her brave honesty. The truth hurt, but it was better than being blinded by a lie. What she didn't know was that, as we hung up the phone, our conversation served as a grave marker for my feelings because that was the night I died inside. The next time he called from college, I broke up with him for good and retreated to my attic sewing room.

BIG CITY WOMAN

By graduation I was sewing well enough to be paid by family and friends. The radio kept me sad company as I worked on my projects, playing songs that kept me pining away at lost love. "Yesterday, all my troubles seemed so far away. Now it looks as though they're here to stay. Oh, I believe in yesterday." I crooned along with the songs of the Beatles and by summer I was living my life facing backwards.

The political protests that were going on during the 1970's helped to validate and energize my own personal rebellion. My regrets about what could have been sent me searching to find happiness beyond home and high school. After working for a year, I saved enough money to go away to college to become a fashion designer. I decided that I had the talent to become great. On that strength, I ignored the objections of my family considering them to be a hindrance to me and huffed off to school.

Once at school, I focused my energies on studying and working on weekends. This experience taught me to be ambitious, independent, and self-reliant. My college counselor recommended that I take a co-op job as an assistant designer in New York for the fall quarter of my senior year. I knew that money was going to be tight, but I took the job to at least try to become famous.

That September, four of us seniors hauled our luggage into a one-bedroom furnished apartment in a well-established New York east side neighborhood. A half-hour subway ride took us just beyond Times Square to the garment district. The showroom for my company was located near Seventh Avenue, otherwise known as "Fashion Avenue." But the design room where I would be working was in a run-down neighborhood between Eighth and Ninth Avenues. There, the drug dealers with flashing eyes and the streetwalkers with gaudy clothes tried to catch people's attention early each morning.

The design room was an unfinished room with high metal beams, a cement floor, a couple of cutting tables, and stacks of cheap cotton material. The fabric must have been the main hiding place for the roaches that scampered across the table every so often as I was cutting samples. The sample pieces were then handed off to four Spanish speaking ladies who sewed on industrial machines that roared.

The designer was Jane, a high-strung, petite strawberry-blonde who seemed to be under a lot of pressure. Her assistant, Kathy, was a recent graduate from our school. No matter how much Kathy spent on clothes, the native New Yorkers in the showroom always reminded her of the heavy, unsophisticated West Virginia accent that betrayed her.

One night, a roommate came home with news about another recent graduate who lost her job because her designer was fired. No wonder Jane was so nervous. With the cost of living so high, this was no city to be stranded without work.

Late one afternoon I made my way back from delivering samples to the showroom. I stepped into the elevator and nodded to the operator, an older foreign-speaking man, who closed the metal gate and cranked the hand lever to take me up to the sixth floor. Something seemed wrong when he cranked the lever again, stopping between floors. Then he turned and stepped towards me. I felt the brush of his fingertips on my neck as he reached to examine the necklace I was wearing. It was a cheap copy of the type of jewelry that Yves St. Laurent was currently showing in Paris that resembled treasure chest coins attached by a chain.

"Are they real?" he asked in low, broken English.

"No, not at all!" I tried to sound casual. "They're just fake!" I was never so glad to be wearing imitation jewelry! His curiosity was satisfied and he turned back to complete the ride. Like a siren going off, something warned me that this man was not at all sincere about high fashion!

With incidents like this and more, this whole trip proved to be much like that coin necklace. Back at school, the teachers had only talked about the "heads" side of the coin—the glamorous, exciting side of fashion. They hadn't told us about the "tails" side. I was discovering that side of the coin for myself.

When I arrived at the design room, I told Jane and Kathy what had just happened. They looked at each other very worried.

"Did he take you to the basement?" they asked.

"No, why?"

"Never mind," they scolded. "Just don't let any of the elevator men take you to the basement!"

Weeks later I was watching the evening news when a picture of my workplace came on the screen. I turned up the sound to hear the story of a pregnant woman who was working there. She had been taken down to the basement and was murdered a year ago. So that's what happened in the basement!

After three long months, the quarter ended and I flew out of New York a few days before Christmas. As the plane banked and spiraled upward, circling the New York vicinity, I was held captive by the glistening view of the lights, buildings, and surrounding water of New York Harbor. I cuddled my portable sewing machine between my feet and whispered my good-byes to Ms. Liberty. The distant sight was impressive. But I knew up close what happens in the streets, the showrooms, and in the elevators. Despite senior year, the "freedom" she represented to pursue a career in fashion design was too high of a price for me to pay.

ALL WORK AND NO PLAY

After graduation, I decided that if the world of Seventh Avenue was not for me, perhaps the corporate world was. I was tired of scrimping and saving throughout college. If I could work for a large company and earn a good salary, then I might find happiness in financial freedom.

With that idea in mind, I interviewed with an employment agency for a retail management position with a national supermarket chain. I knew that the personnel representative would question my switch in career interests, so I faked some strong opinions to try to prove that I was management material. The employment agent was surprised when I got the job, tactlessly letting me know that the company had to meet its minority hiring quota by the end of the year.

For whatever reason I was hired, the challenge of achievement and success appealed to me now. I relocated to another city where I worked at a store close to the downtown area. The long days were filled with grocery truck deliveries, food stamp customers, and union grievances. Sometimes I had to lock up late at night all by myself, walking through an empty parking lot known for trouble.

I developed a mannish temperament to cope with the pressure of pleasing bosses and solving employee problems. I had stepped into a traditionally male position and had to live up to harsh expectations that went against my natural sensitivities. After several years, I learned to talk like a man, dress like a man, and swear like a man.

My behavior began to indicate the anger that had built up inside of me. I had a short fuse and let everyone know it! My zone manager thought he could use my anger to motivate me. He knew that I would muster every muscle to prove I could do something if he insinuated that I couldn't because I was female.

All I was really doing, though, was wearing myself out with overwork. Many times I would call my parents to let them know how I was doing. I told them how I had decorated my apartment and bought a new car. In my spare time, I roamed the malls hungrily searching for something on sale.

"We just want you to be happy," my mother would say. Happiness—what a joke! I gave up on that years ago.

One Sunday I drove to the college town to meet my brother who was in school there. He told me that he had become a Christian and invited me to come with him to church. As I sat in the pew, I stared at the young family in front of us. The father had one arm around his son and lifted his other hand in the air. His posture struck me as being so loving and peaceful as he closed his eyes and sang the hymns. I wondered how he could be so serene.

RUNNING ON EMPTY

Back home I looked around at my apartment and wondered, "Is this it? Isn't there more to life than hard work and a paycheck?" Moreover, I questioned the contrast of my own misery to the sweet contentment of those churchgoers.

My dissatisfaction forced me to look beyond my job for the missing element in my life. I had read several books describing the euphoric high achieved from distance running. For my intensely driven personality, running seemed like the perfect answer. After a few months of running a couple of miles at a steady pace, I was able to identify with what the experts were writing about.

Eventually, I enjoyed feeling the strain on my muscles and the hypnotic beat of my steps striking the concrete. After two years of running, I entered a city-wide race finishing thirteen miles, although I had only practiced for ten. But then, that was my bent—to override my natural abilities and push myself to accomplish my goal.

Soon after the race, my sense of accomplishment vanished, urging me to fill the void with an even higher goal. I signed up for a five mile community run to begin training for a marathon. After about a mile into the race, I had to quit because all my "push" was gone. Strangely, it seemed like I was carrying a bag of concrete inside of my chest. Something had shut down inside of me over which I had no control.

Until this time, I had thought that running was merely a physical exercise controlled by the mind, like the books said. But after experiencing an unexplainable sadness within me, I wondered if there was another part of me that I was not fully aware of. Scared and confused, I left the race knowing that something was really wrong, but without a clue as to what it was.

IS THIS REAL?

One night I talked with my parents, explaining to them how tired and unhappy I was.

"Sweetie, you always have a place here," my dad told me. "Come home."

Going home sounded so good. Within the year I gave up running, resigned from my job, and moved home to Cleveland, Ohio to live with my parents. All this disappointed suburban girl really wanted was to do something meaningful with my life.

That was my intention when I took a job at a commercial photography studio owned by some friends of the family. If I could only use my design background in a creative field, then I would certainly find some deep satisfaction in the pursuit of art! I went to work with that ideal in mind. After a few months of working at the studio,

I noticed that there was something phony and forced about the small family atmosphere.

Relationships were strained because of the owner's wife who made it a practice to apply her psychology degree as she managed the staff. As the business manager, she used a pseudo-parental role by treating people as if they were children, subjecting them to criticism, punishment, and rewards.

I couldn't shake the uneasy, awkward feeling I had facing the daily scrutiny. She would go to lunch with me and ask me personal questions about my family. Then she would apply analysis, talking to me about "self-actualization" which was supposedly the pinnacle goal of self-potential. The psychology sounded good, but its effects produced an atmosphere that seemed almost surrealistic—a distortion of reality. People were merely play-acting their designated roles. I also sensed a volatile undercurrent covered up by a facade of contrived nurturing.

I checked my impressions with another employee and she confided that she was looking for another job. The continual threat of being fired if she didn't measure up was getting to be too much for her. Now the mystery was being unraveled. I detected a self-exalted "Queen Mother" figure who was using her intelligence and authority to control people. I was caught in an unusual sort of company politics where this woman used her knowledge as a manipulative tool to achieve her own self-actualization. As long as we went along with her ideas, she was fine.

Finally, my perceptions were proven to be true. The incident involved the man in charge of the photo lab who was a respected artist in his field. He was an amiable middle-aged bachelor whose hobby was to explore the nuances of fine wine and gourmet cooking. Whatever he did or didn't do that morning caused the business manager to be displeased. Several of us watched as he tried to explain his actions but, unfortunately, confrontation was flowing freely through her veins.

The thin veil of the happy family scenario was quickly thrown off, exposing some long-suppressed tensions. Soon, a full-blown argument was heard echoing from the corners of the studio. The business manager drew a long breath and, like a magical dragon spewing forth fire, burned him with every horrible accusation she could think of. She held nothing back as her criticisms flew with force at the core of his being. We solemnly watched as this 250 lb. man was held speechlessly paralyzed by the raging hatred of a tiny, vengeful woman.

The scene ended with everyone quietly walking away, leaving the lab man to tend to his own wounds. None of us were brave enough to rescue him after what we had just seen. The message was clear—don't ever cross her!

MY EYES WERE OPENED

In the months ahead, I was experiencing more of that shutting down feeling inside. I met with the business manager and we agreed that I should leave because I was not doing well at my job. But before my notice was up, she made it a point to ridicule and embarrass me in front of the staff. I knew what she was capable of, so I handed in my keys and left the studio. I was fed up with her ways and figured she couldn't hurt me anymore if I was gone.

Those encounters with her had triggered questions that had to be answered. I knew that I had witnessed evil. She had purposely used emotional force to harm another person, but where did she get that power? How could the rage of a small woman hold a group of people at bay with such fear? I wanted to know the source of her evil power so that I could get as far away from it as possible.

Somehow I knew that my brother had the answer. I went to visit him and, during that time, asked him matter-of-factly, "Where does evil come from?"

We sat down and he seriously explained that evil power comes from a spirit named Satan who brought sin into the world by tempting man to obtain power for himself. Then his explanation became personal.

"You need to realize that you are a sinner before a holy God." There was nothing I could say. I knew he was telling me the truth.

The present moment melted away as I looked at my past. My eyes were opened to the things I had done and the things that had been done to me. I was deeply ashamed because I knew God had seen them all.

But then my brother went on to say that, because God loves me, He sent his Son, Jesus, to earth to die on a cross, thus paying the substitutionary penalty for my sin. I could receive a full pardon from God if I accepted the work of Christ, turn from my sin, and surrender myself to live for God.

I had been experiencing more of that shutting down feeling accompanied by uncontrollable crying. By now, the feelings were much worse, like light bulbs going out on a string of lights within me.

After clearly hearing what my brother said, I believed that my personal sin was at the very rock bottom of all my problems. As I prayed, I could feel the presence of God in a real way filling me inside, stopping the lights from going completely out. At that moment a silent rescue had taken place. I knew that the Person of Jesus Christ had not only come into my life and forgiven me of my sin, but He had also stopped me from having a nervous breakdown.

MAKING THE TURN

My encounter with Christ was like a cul-de-sac for the road on which I was running; it was a place for me to turn around. As I glanced across the double yellow lines to where I had been, I realized that I had just passed from death to life. In other words, in my sin, I had been suffering from being separated from God in this life, with eventual permanent separation. But in Christ, I had all the benefits of eternal life now and forever. Yielding myself to Jesus was a pivotal moment for me, and I resolved to guard and cherish my relationship with Him always. Having Jesus in my life was more important than having anything else.

Soon, I felt like I wanted to read the Bible. In the Gospels, I was fascinated to observe and learn from the One who had saved me.

Reading through the New Testament, I became acquainted with three major forces that were working against me: the world, the flesh, and the devil. The cumulative effect of these forces easily explained that "bag of concrete" feeling I had in my chest when I was running. God knew the full extent of the damage and was about to begin the repair work necessary. He drew me closer through hours of Bible reading and prayer.

I had been out of work for about six months and had taken a turn for the worse emotionally. My part-time job should have been easy, but the extended unemployment was the proverbial last straw that broke this heavy-laden camel flat on her back in depression.

When the depression came, I could feel something like a dark dense cloud settle over me. Sometimes I would start to go to work and had to turn back because the oppression was so smothering. Some days I could not even get up out of bed.

One warm summer afternoon I was lying down, waiting for the heaviness to subside, when I became aware of my own breathing. As I focused on the up and down motion of my ribcage, my thoughts turned to God. The room became very still and there was an awareness of the space around me, like being the last rider on the bus alone with the driver. As I wondered why God allowed all this to happen to me, I became conscious of His presence. Soon I was engaged in a conversation with Him in my mind.

He showed me that my life was like a single strand of thread and that He was sustaining my fragile breath that very moment. My life was His to control. He had the power to end it, like the snap of a thread, if He willed to do so. Without Him, I would have no breath, no life, nothing.

Then He filled my mind with these words, "You have been doing things your way all your life. Now you are going to do things God's way." His words were not to threaten me but to just state the facts on how things needed to be. Therefore, I was not frightened but respectfully fearful of the complete power He had over me. What He was saying to me was true. My problems in high school, college, and career were due to how I had lived without Him. Now I had to be raised up from the deadening effects of all I had lived through by following my own wrong ways.

I had also seen the results of people using evil power selfishly. My audience with the "Queen Mother" figure at the photography studio showed me that evil resides within people. I had to conclude that evil was also working within me.

Now in Christ, I needed a step-by-step emptying out of the personal sin that had accumulated in my life. That would only happen by carefully following God as He worked to change me. The only way to get out of this depression was to continue to say "Yes" to God as He led me through my own deep, sincere, personal repentance.

∾ Chapter 2 ∾
WHAT ON EARTH IS GOD DOING?

The impact of God's dialogue with me was sobering enough to make me want to listen to Him. Through Bible reading and prayer, God was giving me the emotional healing that I so desperately wanted. I enjoyed a constant sense of His presence and care as He dealt honestly with me. Within a year, my circumstances had improved with a full-time job, a church home, and new Christian friends. In Christ, I had stepped into a realm where God's benevolence was readily available to me and I was glad!

That's why I was so surprised by a friend's comment when I asked her how her life was going with God. I assumed that all Christians were benefiting from God's truth and power in their relationship with Him.

"God's not doin' nothin'!" she said flatly. Laura was a single parent, divorced for about ten years, who wanted in the worst way to be remarried. We had often talked about our desire for marriage, but also compared our similar family backgrounds with alcoholism. I had offered her some books written to explain the resulting effects on alcoholic families, but she refused. She said she didn't see much point in digging up the past.

Judging from her critical attitude, Laura must have felt a lack of closeness to God. Perhaps her refusal to take an honest look at how sin had marred her life had stifled God's movement. He seemed to stop because she had stopped. As I summed up the situation in my mind, I concluded that my friend was locked into a spiritual stand-off with God. Because Laura insisted that God move in a certain way, she was missing the abundant life that Jesus promised when we follow Him. Although she was voicing her perspective, Laura's accusation of God doing nothing was completely untrue.

THE SUPREMACY OF CHRIST

Out of compassion for us, God is continually working to bring aid to people. When it seemed to the Jews that Jesus was breaking the Law by healing a man on the Sabbath, Jesus explained to them, **"My father is always at his work to this very day, and I, too, am working." (John 5:17 NIV)** God has restorative intentions that surpass man's ideas of what is important or good. Out of pure love, God is actively doing an unceasing work beyond the awareness of preoccupied humanity. We would do well to look past our personal concerns long enough to find out for ourselves, "What on earth is God doing?"

To answer that question, we need to peer into His everlasting point of view. A broad overview of God's work is given to us in the book of Colossians. **"He** (Christ) **is the image of the invisible God… all things were created by him and for him. He is before all things, and in him all things hold together…so that in everything he** (Christ) **might have the supremacy." (Colossians 1:15-20 NIV)** The Father's work upon the earth is that of Christ regaining supremacy in all aspects of the fallen, runaway creation. The basis for this work is the provision for man to be reconciled to God through the shed blood of Jesus for sin. As people receive God's forgiveness through Christ, their relationship with God is restored. Then their lives can be changed from a loathsome expression of sin to a glorification of God as God originally intended. The invisible God can duplicate His image in people when Christ reigns supreme in them. God's power is seen when human nature is radically changed to mirror God's divine nature. Transformation of sin-filled lives by asserting Christ's supremacy is the essence of the Father's work upon the earth.

The Father is working to express himself through individuals, but also through a body of people which is the Church. As Head of all those who are established in God, Jesus works by His Spirit in us, around us, and through us to further the purposes of God. For example, He works in us to change the way we think and act so that we will reveal Christ in our behavior. He works around us to bring solutions to our problems and relief from our difficulties. And He works through us by moving us to communicate the Gospel to others, along with expressions of love and good deeds. In us, around us, and through us—Christ is doing the Father's work always.

THE SIN BARRIER

Unfortunately, as in Laura's case, we can see God's work effectively being blocked. This is the work of sin in our lives. Sin forms a barrier in us that obstructs God's revealed glory. **"Rather, your iniquities have been barriers between you and your God..." (Isaiah 59:2 NRSV)** The work of sin goes against what God is doing. Sin opposes the supremacy of Christ.

God's persistence in His work stems from His mercy towards us. He wants to spare us from sin's harm, knowing that sin brings only death, destruction, and separation from God. The Father was willing to pay the ultimate price, the life of His only Son, in order to break sin's power over us. **"Grace and peace to you from God our Father, and the Lord Jesus Christ, who gave himself for our sins to rescue us from the present evil age, according to the will of our God and Father..." (Galatians 1:3-4 NIV)** The severity of the sacrifice of Christ is the most compelling argument to our hearts against sin. The love act of Christ's death was intended to turn us towards God and away from sin.

The work of Christ's supremacy is meant to bring us close to God. The more we are surrendered to Christ, the greater the reconciliation and more closely united we are to Him. The Father's loving goal is to be close to His children.

CONTAINERS BY DESIGN

We are wonderfully designed in a special way to express God's glory. We were created as "vessels" or "containers" to carry God's presence. God chose to display His power by re-making us inwardly and then releasing His presence to emanate from us. The Apostle Paul explained that he was merely a carrier of the divine presence when he wrote, **"But we have this treasure in jars of clay to show that this all-surpassing power is from God and not from us." (2 Corinthians 4:7 NIV)**

Our physical body is merely a clay pot which holds the contents of the human soul and spirit. We have the capacity to be filled up and the ability to be emptied out. This inner being, also called the inner man, is the part of us in which God wants to achieve supremacy. **"Love the Lord your God with all your heart and with all your soul and with all your mind." (Matthew 22:37 NIV)** Our outward physical behavior will follow the moves of our inner man.

But the inner man is also where the sin barriers exist. Sin clogs the "container" by its opposition to the flow of God's life within us. Sin issues accumulate from living in a fallen world. From childhood, people take in a vast amount of input that leaves an impression on the inner being. If these impressions from a corrupt world are not somehow purged, we become loaded with them.

Of course, we are not merely passive receivers, but also active participants in sinful acts. Yes, situations have marred us, but we have done more than our fair share of filling our containers with the wrong things!

With this in mind, let's look at several different aspects of the work of sin in order to become fully convinced of our personal need of Christ's supremacy.

∿ Chapter 3 ∿
SIN'S TRIPLE PUNCH

The Bible describes three major forces that negatively influence all people: the world, the flesh, and the devil. These forces bring pressure upon us to sin against God. A brief account of their impact upon the individual is given in the book of Ephesians. **"As for you, you were dead in your transgressions and sins, in which you used to live when you followed the ways of this world and of the ruler of the kingdom of the air, the spirit who is now at work in those who are disobedient." (Ephesians 2:1-3 NIV)**

These forces all work together in their rebellion against God, therefore, they are intertwined and not totally distinct. One expert on spiritual warfare writes, "While it is helpful to see our sin problem from three dimensions, it is also problematic. Sin is too dynamic (in the negative sense) to be compartmentalized."[1] With this caution in mind, let's look at each force separately in order to see how we have suffered from its influence in our inner man.

THE WORLD

The "world" can be defined as the inhabited earth and system of living that was corrupted by sin, empowered by rebellion, and moving in opposition to God. It is the collective efforts of the creature (man) turning away from his Creator to actively pursue and apprehend a portion of the creation for himself.

---

1   The Handbook of Spiritual Warfare, p. 102

The "ways of the world" are the practices used by people to get along in this system. Energized by greed, people are set on getting something for themselves by whatever means they feel necessary. They see the world as a yummy pie and are willing to do what it takes to get a big, juicy slice. **"...For all that is in the world—the desire of the flesh, the desire of the eyes, the pride in riches— comes not from the Father but from the world." (1 John 2:16 NRSV)**

The world is an evil force because, like stepping onto an escalator moving downward away from God, people get carried away. We easily become filled with desire for the physical enhancements of life because we enjoy pointing to things and saying "MINE"! The hunger for one more gadget, one more matching outfit, one more ring for one more finger has a way of turning the extras into essentials for us. Owning material possessions can become so important to us that the last thing we would want to hear about is the supremacy of Christ!

The spiritual danger of the world lies in its power to distract us from God. The Bible pictures the world as the city of Babylon. **"Woe! Woe, O great city, O Babylon, city of power!" (Revelation 18:10 NIV)** This city lures us to commit our lives to its countless occupations, pleasures, hobbies, trends, education, philosophies, and causes. Like the gravitational pull upon the earth that keeps us earthbound, so does the corrupted world have a pull on the heart of man to keep him involved with the many activities around him. This subtle, unseen force is described this way: "**By your magic spell all nations were led astray." (Revelation 18:23 NIV)**

The world vies for our precious time as we become preoccupied with its array of choices. When we are caught up in its demands, our resources are spent on everything but God. Our time, energy, money, talents, learning abilities, goals, and dreams are squandered on this passing life rather than invested in eternal purposes.

God's main concern with worldly pursuits is that they compete with our relationship with Him. Christians who commit themselves in the world's activities involve themselves in a love relationship different from God. Scripture states this clearly: **"Adulterers! Do you not know that friendship with the world is enmity with God? Therefore whoever wishes to be a friend of the world becomes an enemy of God. Or do you suppose that it is for nothing that Scripture says, 'God yearns jealously for the spirit that he has made to dwell in us'?" (James 4:4-5 NRSV)** A friend is someone with whom we relate well and enjoy spending time with. The friendship grows as more time is spent together. The more friends understand each other, the deeper the union becomes. God is saying that His jealousy is aroused because He has made it possible for His Holy Spirit to dwell in us and we ignore Him! We run off, like adulterers, and spend our love on the world. God is extremely concerned when His Christians relate better to a corrupted world that to His eternal Holy Spirit.

The Commodore One such a man who gave himself fully to this world's temporary achievements was "Commodore" Cornelius Vanderbilt. He died in 1877 as the richest man in America, leaving an astronomical $105 million to his heirs. As a young man, his zeal for business made him a fortune in the shipping industry. His first break came when his mother loaned him $100 to operate a ferryboat on the New York waterways. His interests eventually turned to railroads. That enterprise doubled his worth in the last twenty years of his life. The Commodore expressed his affection for the world's opportunities when he said, "I have been insane on the subject of making money all my life."[2]

By 1890, the Vanderbilt heirs, along with other successful opportunists, christened a period of American history called "The Gilded Age." The name referred to a time of opulence and furious fortune spending. The society papers raved about the fancy dress balls and other doings given by this new American aristocracy, while the lower classes looked on. There seemed to be no end to the accumulation of New York City mansions, ocean front summer homes, yachts, jewelry, art, and world treasures.

---

2   Fortune's Children, p.27

America's wealth became so concentrated within this elitist group that an estimated 9 percent of the nation's families controlled 11 percent of the nation's wealth.[3] This era was so "pregnant" with materialism that it gave birth to "The American Dream" which is the hope in our free society to someday go from rags to riches.

Today, this hope remains strong, luring people into believing that, with the right breaks or the right lottery number, they, too, can become millionaires. At the very least, "The American Dream" has set a precedent for material prosperity in our country that seems rightfully ours.

To clarify this, I am not saying that it is wrong to have a good job, make a good buck, or inherit wealth. I am simply pointing out the frantic pursuit of the upscale lifestyle in our culture as opposed to the pursuit of Christ. Shopping is all around us, and we can easily assume that God's revealed glory is the American lifestyle. But God has a different opinion of what is glorious, and we need to find out what His opinion is. **"But seek first his kingdom and his righteousness, and all these things will be given to you as well." (Matthew 6:33 NIV)**

Moses

We would do well to learn from the life of Moses who, like Cornelius Vanderbilt, had the chance to gain the world's wealth for himself in his youth. As the adopted son of Egypt's Pharaoh, worldly glory was well within his reach. But instead of lusting after the world's treasures, he longed for the higher ways of God. **"He regarded disgrace for the sake of Christ as of greater value than the treasures of Egypt, because he was looking ahead to his reward." (Hebrews 11:26 NIV)**

Forty years spent as a lowly shepherd in the desert sufficiently stripped Moses of his egotistical ways. The sacrifice of personal greatness made him a qualified vessel by which God could display His splendor. God used Moses to perform supernatural acts of power to rescue a whole nation from its oppressors. With greater

---

3   Fortune's Children, p.264

vision than any industrialist, God had set His sights on gaining a people for Himself and testifying of His greatness to the other nations of the world.

Moses' life was totally used up in achieving God's purposes. As an old man, Moses reflected on his life and said, **"I have become an alien in a foreign land." (Exodus 18:3 NIV)** The world's enticements were strange and unfamiliar to Moses. The world was not his friend, nor his god. Instead, Moses had spent his life gazing into the face of God until God had become his world. What better way could we spend our life than seeking Christ for His supremacy?

THE FLESH

The second influence we contend with as humans is the "flesh" or "self-life." When we do not allow Christ to reign supreme, then self will reign instead. For instance, written in black marker on a splintered bus stop bench were the words, "Ryan Peters Rules!" The "little ruler" of self has instinctively begun to mark out his territory. Ryan Peters is warming up to the belief that he rules his own life, the bus stop, and to some degree, the world.

By nature, we are self-centered. This means that we automatically see ourselves as being in the middle, with everything revolving around us. With this orientation, we see life through "self-colored glasses" and expect everything to be ordered as we want to have it.

When we become absorbed in ourselves, we are less concerned about God and others. This is like a man walking into a deep, dark tunnel. As he goes in, the light of his conscience towards others grows dimmer and dimmer. Instead of heeding the warning of the diminishing light, the man keeps going as his eyes adjust to the dark. After a while, he has no awareness of the harm he is causing others by his selfishness because he is so enveloped in his own wants and needs. **"They are darkened in their understanding and separated from the life of God because of the ignorance that is in them due to the hardening of their hearts." (Ephesians 4:18 NIV)** Potentially, self can become our world.

The main temptation of the flesh is in living for the stimulation of our physical body. Basically, we live to please ourselves. For example, when I was running, I thought I needed the sense of accomplishment from the road races. I also became hooked on the physical exercise. I enjoyed the sensation of strength in my muscles because it made me feel powerful and in control, and I began to live for those feelings. People can be so eager to have their felt needs met that they launch themselves into excesses beyond good reason. This explains our propensity for addictions and obsessions. **"The one who sows to please his sinful nature, from that nature will reap destruction…" (Galatians 6:8 NIV)**

Attempts to satisfy unmet emotional needs can be especially destructive. People will sometimes do anything for love, or at least have something that feels like love. They may also strive to feel important, feel powerful, feel superior, or feel desirable. Women's clothing today is designed for those who feel the need to draw attention to themselves. One of the works of the flesh in women is the sense of power they gain from being able to attract men by the way they look.

The flesh is harder to understand as an agent of sin because it is within us and, therefore, seems normal. We can easily understand how violence in society is wrong, but seeing our own inner violence is a much harder truth to swallow. Unfortunately, when we sympathize with the voice of self and do whatever we want, we easily slip into depravity. **"Furthermore, since they did not think it worthwhile to retain the knowledge of God, he gave them over to a depraved mind…they have become filled with every kind of wickedness… full of envy, murder, strife, deceit and malice…they invent ways of doing evil." (Romans 1:28-30 NIV)** The voice of self shouts its demands, "I want! I will! I won't!" as the inner taskmaster drives our body, mind, and emotions on a detour away from God.

Someone Is At The Door!

The only way to hush the voice of self is to hearken to the voice of God. By His guidance, we can be led out of the tunnel of self.

"Here I am! I stand at the door and knock. If anyone hears my voice and opens the door, I will come in and eat with him, and he with me." (Revelation 3:20 NIV) When I read this verse, I picture a lonely person who has turned inward and locked himself into a tiny closet of self.

Then a knock comes from the other side as a friendly voice beckons. The trapped person reaches for the door handle and gives it a turn. In steps Jesus who helps him straighten up.

He leads that person to a well lit dining hall where others are seated around a table. Without losing that special relationship with Jesus, that person sees that he's not the only one. He realizes that other people have needs also, and that some have even greater needs than him. Now sharing freely among friends, he says to himself, "How could I have been so stubborn to spend my life in that closet? Thank you, Jesus, for leading me out of ME!"

THE DEVIL

We now consider the third aspect of this rather ominous portrait of self-willed man operating in a corrupt world system directed by the devil. There are two main truths about the devil that we must believe. The first is that he is completely REAL!

Our cultural rationalism tends to wave a sophisticated hand at supernatural evil, passing it off as make-believe. Feeling safe with that presumption, Americans then explore unknown spiritual realms through astrologers, psychics, and fortune-tellers. In his book *Unholy Spirits*, occult expert Gary North makes this observation: "Western rationalism has always had a kind of alliance with Western irrationalism."[4] In other words, Americans reason away hell and yet ponder its possibilities. True demonic activity is then perceived as a frightful, yet fascinating game. But Biblical reality shows that satanic evil reaching into people's lives is no game.

The second truth for us to know is that the devil is ANGRY! The devil has been judged by God for his sin in Heaven and is waiting for his sentence to be carried out. While he waits, the devil is taking

---

4 Unholy Spirits, p. 144

his revenge. Since God is beyond his reach, he takes his fury out on God's most prized creation—that's US!

The devil knows that hurting us pains God because God created man to enter into a love relationship with Him. The devil sets himself as man's supreme enemy who continually plans for our destruction. **"The thief comes only to steal, kill and destroy." (John 10:10 NIV)**

His primary work is to keep people from a restored relationship with God. He knows that when a person responds to God's saving grace, the Holy Spirit will then work to produce the character of Christ in him. The devil dreads seeing replicas of Christ walking the earth. To prevent that, he works to cause damage to man's inner being. He attempts to fill our containers with as much sin and hurt as possible to deaden us so that we will not respond to God.

What makes the devil so deadly is that he is so subtle. Most of the time we don't even recognize him because his work is so veiled. **"Now the serpent was more crafty than any of the wild animals..." (Genesis 3:1NIV)** Let's go on with a more in-depth study of the devil's work so that we might assess the possible damage he has done to our inner being.

↝ Chapter 4 ↜
WE KNOW HIS SCHEMES

An invisible enemy has a definite advantage over us. An invisible enemy with supernatural intelligence has an even greater advantage. The Apostle Paul discerned the devil's cunning schemes among new believers and, as a preventive measure, taught at length about Christian living. The key to recognizing the devil's work is to understand the Bible's offer of life in Christ.

LIES

One scheme that the devil uses against us is to constantly speak lies to our minds. **"When he lies, he speaks his native language, for he is a liar and the father of lies." (John 8:44 NIV)** Like a mole digging underground, the devil is at work with lies to uproot our belief system. Just as the crooked pattern of uplifted dirt leaves the lawn in need of repair, lies spoken to a person's mind will distort what he believes to be true. Belief is a critical part of our spiritual life because we come to know Christ simply by believing in Him. If our belief system has been distorted by lies, then our perception of God will need repair. Knowing Christ closely depends on believing Him fully.

I witnessed the devil at work with his lying thoughts one day while driving my friend's children home from a weekend stay. Six year old Trisha was next to me in the front seat of the car. As we talked, she suddenly changed the subject and repeated what she was hearing in a puppet-like way.

"I know more than my dad!"

"Trisha, no you don't," I said gently. "Your dad is very smart." She didn't answer. The look on her face told me that she wasn't quite convinced; the lying thought had been firmly planted in her mind.

When I dropped the kids off at home, her dad met her with a hug and told her how much he missed her. A big, secure smile beamed across her face. The lying thought must have vanished, disproven by a very smart dad.

In this instance, the lie Satan had whispered was detected and dispelled. But how many of his lies have we accepted into our thought life as being true? The devil's suggestions bring us doubt, worry, suspicion of others, and pride. He tells us lies about best friends, relatives, and church leaders. Paul wrote to the Corinthians warning them about the divisions among them. The devil, no doubt, had tempted believers with envious comparisons in their minds. He knows that if he can incite us into attacking each other, we will stay busy struggling in our personal relationships and will be out of step with how God is moving.

FEAR

We all have an intuitive, rational fear to avoid danger, but the devil uses lies to instill fear that is irrational and overwhelming. Fear is the devil's "stun-gun" to paralyze human behavior. If a person is afraid of something, he will stop and go no further. That person is robbed of the personal freedom of exploring his potential in Christ. The following is an example of how fear effectively controls behavior.

A policeman, moonlighting as a substitute teacher, was hired to teach at a junior high school. He was scheduled to teach first period English and second period Math. With writing as his hobby, he felt that the English class would be a breeze, but he struggled with Math and hoped for the best.

When he arrived at school he was excited to pour himself into the English class. Instead, he spent the hour trying to make the kids stay in their seats and pay attention. The academic nightmare was over when the bell rang.

Anticipating the same trouble with the Math class, he put the whole lesson on the board between classes. He noticed that most of the same kids came back into the room for second period. This time, the class was quite different. The students sat quietly in their seats and listened to every word.

Puzzled, the teacher asked them, "Do you have any questions you would like to ask me?" One student meekly raised his hand.

"Do you always bring a gun to school when you substitute?"

A few students had seen the gun in the policeman's shoulder holster when he raised his arm to write the lesson on the board. They warned the rest of the class, and the "fear of death" froze them in their seats!

The fear of death speaks universally to the heart of man. The devil holds the whole world at spiritual "gun-point" with the threat of death while suppressing the truth about Christ's victory over death. The fear of death is a very successful scheme that the devil uses to keep people in emotional bondage. But the power of the threat of death was broken by Christ's resurrection. **"We know that Christ, being raised from the dead, will never die again; death no longer has dominion over him." (Romans 6:9 NRSV)** Knowing that Christ overcame death releases us from being held hostage by fear.

VIOLENCE

The devil also attempts to fill our lives with violence by inciting one person against another. The Apostle Paul exposed this work of Satan when he wrote: **"Put on the full armor of God so that you can take your stand against the devil's schemes. For our struggle is not against flesh and blood…" (Ephesians 6:11-12 NIV)** He was warning us not to act upon thoughts against others suggested to us by demonic forces.

Spiritual freedom expert Dr. Neil Anderson reports from a survey taken among 1,725 teenagers attending evangelical schools: "70 percent had heard 'voices' in their heads as if a subconscious self talked to them or they really struggled with bad thoughts, 20 percent frequently entertained thoughts of suicide, and 24 percent had impulsive thoughts to kill someone…"[5] If these statistics represent the normal thought life of Christian kids, one can just imagine the thoughts in the minds of unbelievers who may act upon them with no restraint.

The devil knows that if he can get us into the habit of becoming angry about personal offenses and then dwell on those feelings, he will have a foothold. If anger is not resolved with communication and forgiveness, then all he has to do is tend the fire by adding more offenses. We make life miserable for others when anger rages within us. **"Do not let the sun go down while you are still angry and do not give the devil a foothold." (Ephesians 4:26 NIV)**

Unresolved anger leads to feelings of murder that make us want to kill someone for what they did. Because murder is illegal, people normally downshift their violence by finding discreet ways such as harsh words and body language to convey their feelings. These ways are effective in communicating our interpersonal violence.

Our natural tendency is to want revenge to pay back harm for what we have suffered. Much child abuse today is due to adults acting on unresolved anger. For example, a baby-sitter was found physically abusing a boy while under her care. It was later found that she had an abusive father whom she hated. The feelings of revenge she had for her father were somehow soothed by taking action against that child.[6] We can easily see from today's headlines how the devil incites men, women, and children against each other, filing lives with anger, hatred, revenge, and violence.

RELIGION

Yet another scheme used against us is religion, which looks good at first glance. Religion about God is the devil's substitute for relationship with God. It is following rules about Jesus rather than following Jesus as He rules.

Religious man tries to impress God with his works to try to convince God to accept him. Righteous man, however, comes to God

---

5   Helping Others Find Freedom In Christ, p. 27
6   *The Plain Dealer*, August 6, 1996

empty-handed and accepts what Christ has done on his behalf. I remember my grandfather's comment one time as we drove past an orthodox church with a huge gold-plated dome.

"That ought to impress Christ!" he said emphatically.

Months later as we sat together watching a televised Billy Graham Crusade, he met God on His terms by receiving Christ as Savior. The devil's work of man-made religion was replaced by Christ-made relationship.

The strategy against us in religion is to make us feel satisfied with our own methods of morality. Then we will not sense our need to go to God personally. Our religious practices keep God at arm's length while we assume that what we have formed will win God's approval. Deceptive religious teaching is very prevalent in our society as people seek to fill their spiritual void. Here are some common examples.

Basically Good

One of the most accepted religious lies that distorts our belief system originates from humanism which is the deification of man. The belief that man is basically good denies the truth about our basic sin nature. In our own estimation, our actions don't really seem too bad. Disbelief in personal sin gives us a "Pollyanna" perspective that being nice is good enough to live by.

"As long as we are nice and help each other then we will go to Heaven," explained a woman who had recently moved to this country from the ex-Soviet Union. I mentioned to her that I was a Christian and began to explain some facts about Jesus Christ. She signaled me with her eyes to drop the subject. When we ignore the truth about our own wrongdoing, then we are the ones who are **"pure in their own eyes, yet not washed from their filthiness." (Proverbs 30:12 NRSV)**

This religious concept is widespread because it originated in the Garden of Eden and continued on. Man and woman ate from the tree of the knowledge of good and evil, and **"...the eyes of both of them were opened..." (Genesis 3:7 NIV)** In one bite, they acquired

31

a working knowledge of how to do good and how to do evil. As a result, we know how to act nice and we know how to get nasty. We can clean up our appearance and act innocent no matter what horrible things we have said or how much wrong we have done.

We tell ourselves, "I am such a loving person. I would NEVER do anything like that!" These inner compliments admit to only looking at the "good" side of our basic nature. How many times have we heard people say, "That's MY way of showing love!" when actually they were doing harm? Our reasoning can become so mixed up that we call evil "good" and good "evil." Refusing to admit evil intentions while faking a decent cover-up enables us to keep self intact. This knowledge is the basis for all pretense.

If a Christian holds to the idea that he is "basically good" even with the understanding of the necessity of Jesus' sacrifice for sin, then religious deception has distorted his beliefs. He will not see the whole scope of his sin as religious pride blocks the Holy Spirit from revealing the true contents of the heart.

We need to rid ourselves of humanistic thinking by fully accepting the fact that people are basically sinful. **"For all have sinned and fall short of the glory of God…" (Romans 3:23 NIV)** Our relief is in the fact that Christ saves us from our sin. To believe any other premise plays right into the scheme of self-satisfied religion.

Positive Thinking

Another popular religious teaching is "Positive Thinking." This is the practice of training our mind to only look at the "positive" side of life with the hopes of a resulting favorable outcome. But it is also an exercise in resisting what we prefer not to think about.

What began as a "look on the bright side" training to help people overcome feelings of inferiority has evolved into "mind over matter" doctrine. Dr. Norman Vincent Peale discovered his ability to manage his thought life by an act of his will. He formed a discipline to accept, reject, or build upon his own personal system of thoughts. He documented his discovery in his famous classic *The*

Power of Positive Thinking, which begins: "Believe in yourself! Have faith in your own abilities!"[7]

As motivating as this may sound, Dr. Peale unfortunately steers his readers into a man-centered religion rather than a Christ-centered relationship. I say this for several reasons. First, his teaching puts emphasis on having success in this life. The eternal goal of storing up riches in Heaven is not presented. Instead, the reader is given a way to have all he desires. "Self-confidence leads to self-realization and successful achievement."[8]

Second, Dr. Peale urges us to be adamant about what we want in life. "Formulate and stamp indelibly on your mind a mental picture of yourself succeeding. Hold this picture tenaciously. Never permit it to fade…"[9] We see a striking contrast in this advice to Peter's counsel to struggling Christians: **"Humble yourselves, therefore, under God's mighty hand, that he may lift you up in due time." (1 Peter 5:6 NIV)** Dr. Peale goes on to explain that, once we determine in our mind what we want, we will eventually get what we see ourselves as having. This is basic visualization technique that is so popular in New Age religion.

Next, Scripture is reduced to a strategy for success. "I shall give you a formula which will work if you use it."[10] He recommends reciting certain verses ten times per day until our confidence builds. Rather than read Scripture to meet Jesus, the author offers to get us through our next sales appointment. In other words, God is not sought—He is summoned!

Finally, we are told that with the right outlook, God will work for us. The Person of the Holy Spirit is reduced to a cosmic energy to be unleashed in our circumstances. The power in "Positive Thinking" seems to be man training his mind to believe that God will follow him through life, endorsing every wish. This is totally backwards.

---

7   The Power of Positive Thinking, p. 6

8   Ibid, p. 1

9   Ibid, p. 13

10   Ibid, p. 25

Dr. Peale's methods have had a tremendous influence, laying the groundwork for many "Positive Mental Attitude" teachers today. Despite its popularity, this man-made form of thought control needs to be questioned for its true spiritual value.

What happens when God wants to deal with us about sin? Would we resist conviction because it is too negative? When Christ begins to require self-sacrifice of us, would we refuse to serve because it doesn't meet our criteria for a successful life? We need to re-think this avenue of super-achieve-ism as it compares to the achievement of Christ's supremacy over us. What may seem to be a useful tool for daily living may actually thwart God's higher purposes for us.

Steps Doctrine

Another way God is being packaged these days is through "Steps" doctrine. This teaching lays out a number of spiritual-sounding rules to be memorized and followed. Supposedly, if people adhere to these rules, they can stave off harmful behavior habits. An appeal is made to a "Higher Power" for intervention, but concentration is on the habit, not God Himself. So with "Steps" doctrine, man determines what God should do by assigning Him a task to perform.

Here is an example of how this religious teaching fails. A girl-friend told me about a weekend she went on a "spiritual retreat."

"What did they teach you at the retreat?" I asked.

"They taught us how to handle situations in life," she told me. Then she went on to repeat each of the steps she had learned, or at least the ones she could remember.

As we talked, she confided that she had just gone through a very upsetting time. The man she had been dating went with her to get her car fixed. He didn't like the way she was handling the nego-tiations with the mechanic, so he struck her with his elbow. She was shocked at first, but then disheartened because of her history with abusive relationships.

"At the time he struck you," I said, "which of the twelve steps did you recall to help you?"

She drew a blank.

"I couldn't think of anything. I was too surprised and hurt. I felt like crying."

I explained that a personal relationship with Jesus could have prevented that from happening. Because He loves us, He wants to steer us away from harmful relationships. In the presence of evil, we need a Person with power to call upon, not steps to remember.

In the book *The Useful Lie*, the author examines "Steps" doctrine step-by-step and concludes: "The world, whether it be in the form of Twelve Stepdom or any other system, does not have the answer. Jesus Christ is the answer."[11]

If we truly want to change, then we need to allow God to make changes as He sees fit, knowing that His changes may clash with what we want to hold on to. Dr. Billy Graham writes, "No amount of self-improvement or wishful thinking can change a man's basic nature. Only God—the One who created us—can re-create us."[12]

Liar-Liar

With religion, man is empowered by knowledge rather than by the Holy Spirit. His religious pride causes him to love his intellect rather than the One who loved him first. As he cherishes his religious systems, man is proud about what he knows rather than be humbled before Who he knows.

In the Garden, man made a fatal trade when he followed the devil's suggestions to disobey God. Satan enticed man with religion to make his own way to God knowing full well that the form was empty and useless to restore relationship. With man at a distance from God, the enemy was then able to carry out his subtle revenge tactics.

A close relationship with Christ is our advantage over an unseen, intelligent, hostile enemy. **"The Lord is my rock, and my fortress, and my deliverer; my God, my strength, in who I will trust; my**

11 The Useful Lie, p. 115
12 The Holy Spirit, p. 51

**buckler, and the horn of my salvation, and my high tower."
(Psalm 18:2 KJV)** With Christ as our "hide-out" and our "look-out", He will warn us, protect us, intervene, out-maneuver, and over-power our personal enemy every time.

∾ Chapter 5 ∾
THE VERY THING I DO NOT WISH

Having examined the three major spiritual forces—the world, the flesh, and the devil—we can begin to see how we have been adversely affected. But there are other aspects of sin that we should also be aware of because they compound our problem.

The Apostle Paul painstakingly describes our struggle with the power of sin in the book of Romans chapter seven. He explains that man's mortal body is a prisoner and sin is its "jailer." People go through life doing bad things that they really don't want to do, but have no power not to. People with no understanding of God can really get themselves into a jam because sin automatically leads them towards behavior that is detrimental.

But thanks to God, through Christ man no longer has to obey sin as it directs, but can live according to the Spirit's guidance. The Spirit has the power to disengage sin's power over us.

The key to coming out of sin's grasp is having the awareness of what sin is making us do that is contrary to God. The more we realize how sin is working in us, the more its grip can be broken and we can walk free. This is the victorious life available to us in Christ. Let's go on to be free!

SIN IS SECRETIVE

The immediate result from eating forbidden fruit in the Garden was that man thought he could successfully hide from an all-knowing God. With the knowledge of good and evil, man's abilities seemed great to him. He chose to believe in his own thoughts rather than what he knew to be true about God. The first work of sin was for man to exalt his own thinking above true reality. Much of what we think in our mind seems more real to us than the truth.

The second work of sin was for man to become secretive about his actions. Sin took up residence within man's heart as a closely guarded secret, protected by human reasoning. In his effort to hide from God, man did not know that he was only hiding from himself. God knew what man had done, but man refused to admit the truth about his own actions. Self-deception has us believing the cover-up lies we tell ourselves in preference to the truth.

Picture the ostrich hiding from her pursuer by burying her head in the sand. Gripped by fear of being caught, she thinks that, because her eyes are covered, no one can see her. She believes she is hiding in darkness when, in fact, she is standing in full view!

With self-deception, we behave the same way. In truth, we all live our lives before God. **"For a man's ways are in full view of the Lord, and he examines all his paths." (Proverbs 5:21 NIV)** We think that, because we have been secretive, no one sees. Sin is hidden from our view in the darkness of denial. Perhaps our secrets have been buried for so long we don't remember all we have hidden. But rather than face God and allow Him to bring the truth to light, we keep our eyes covered, hiding from God like the ostrich.

WE LOVE OUR SIN

Despite Paul's brilliant expose' of the work of sin, many times we remain its prisoner. Why? Because we love our sin! At conversion, when Christ reveals Himself to the heart, a new believer is faced with the decision to either love or leave his sin. If we love God's way and choose to leave sin, then we need to resolve to leave it completely. This is not easy because our love for sin is so great.

Lot and his wife were two people torn between loves while they lived in Sodom. When the city was about to be destroyed for its wickedness, the angels urged Lot and his family to flee for their lives. Lot hesitated and had to be physically dragged away to be saved. Later,

THE VERY THING I DO NOT WISH

his wife had her own regrets and, while looking back, became a pillar of salt. As evil as their environment was, they still couldn't stand to part with it. The thought of leaving sin habits makes us sad, like losing a life-long companion. Leaving sin is like the parting of two lovers tightly embraced. Sin becomes so much a part of us that we cannot imagine life without it.

We love our sin mainly because it helps us get our own way. The element of power in sin attracts us to use sinful ways to get what we want. For instance, if we learn that losing our temper leaves people cowering or that complaining coerces others to give in to us, then these ways have proven useful to us.

There is also pleasure in sin. We wouldn't commit sin if it weren't, to some extent, fun. We enjoy the way it stimulates our flesh and excites our emotions. Producers of movies capitalize on our appetite for emotionalism with the shows they offer. We watch television dramas because many of us just love a good fight! Their provocative dialogues thrill us with each sin-filled scene!

We live out our own soap-opera scenes, too. For example, one day at work I watched as a woman refused to answer the salesman's questions because she didn't like him. When he brought the forms back later, they were filled out wrong and had to be re-signed by the customer. The woman seized the moment to magnify the error; her screams were heard throughout the whole office. After he left, I glanced over and saw an unmistakable smile on her face. Her lips were practically smacking at the pain and embarrassment she had just caused him. She had purposely set him up, and now she was immersed in the afterglow of the pleasure of her sin.

The Bible describes our love of sin: **"Though evil is sweet in his mouth and he hides it under his tongue, though he cannot bear to let it go and keeps it in his mouth, yet his food will sour in his stomach; it will become the venom of serpents." (Job 20:12-14 NIV)**

Sinful pleasure seems to have a temporary "Band-Aid" affect on our flesh; for a time it covers the ache in our soul. The temptation to sin is always within easy grasp as a possible solution to our problems. Alcohol, drugs, immorality, over-spending, over-eating, even over-sleeping all bring a type of relief from harsh reality. Sin seems like an easy way out, but it only further complicates life. So we are faced with the daily choice to either enjoy the short-lived pleasure of sin or enjoy right fellowship with God.

SIN BLINDS US

Many times we need to be shown or told what we are doing wrong because we just don't see it. Sin "blinds" us so that we view life from our own sinful perspective. For example, I remember driving through the mountains on the West Virginia Turnpike and hitting a dense patch of fog. Suddenly, we could barely see the hood of our car because there was zero visibility. Our only hope of driving safely on that mountain road was to eventually come out of the fog. Self-deception and falsehood cause us to travel along in a similar spiritual condition. By leaving sin to follow God's truth, we can come out of the "fog" to better distinguish reality.

We are especially blind to our sin when we have acted wrongly without correction. We get into habits of behavior that seem normal to us. In his book *The Lies We Believe*, Dr. Chris Thurman writes, "some of the lies we tell ourselves we know to be lies…some we believe have actually become 'truth' because we have practiced them for so long. These are the most dangerous lies of all because we rarely, if ever, dispute them. We don't dispute what we believe to be true."[13]

The Bible expresses the same idea this way, **"For as he thinketh in his heart, so is he." (Proverbs 23:7 KJV)** Whatever we think in our heart, we will live out. Words that express what we think, we will speak out. Simply put, we act upon what we think, so the key to our living is our thinking.

God's remedy for sin-filled thinking is the renewing of our minds. Our point of view needs to be replaced by God's perspective as revealed through Scripture. In my own life, many of my emotional problems were relieved when I changed my mind and

---

13   The Lies We Believe, p. 34

accepted what the Bible was telling me. This simple solution is possible for anyone.

Let's look at three common thinking habits that blind us from seeing our own behavior.

Blame-shifting

Blame-shifting is our quick response to push blame onto something or someone else at the discovery of our sin. It is the knee-jerk reaction of finding an object for our excuse. We use this reasoning to get the heat off of self while ducking the truth, thus avoiding the personal responsibility and consequences of our sin.

The habitual use of these excuses causes us to have a victim attitude. We see everyone else as the aggressor and we are just poor, innocent victims. Blame-shifting is a selfish assumption that the fault lies with everyone else. We don't consider ourselves to be part of the problem.

We react this way because we are afraid of facing the truth. When the fear of humiliation is greater than our desire for truth, we will use this device to protect ourselves. We may dread what other people will think or perhaps we fear facing who we really are, avoiding it at all cost. **"Everyone who does evil hates the light, and will not come into the light for fear that his deeds will be exposed." (John 3:20 NIV)**

The habit of blame-shifting originated in the Garden of Eden when God questioned man about his disobedience. **"The woman you put here with me—she gave me some fruit from the tree and I ate it." (Genesis 3:12 NIV)** The woman caught on quickly and shifted her blame to the serpent. We can almost hear their minds racing as they used their newly acquired knowledge to escape personal accountability to God.

After centuries, we continue to do the same thing. An article in the women's section of the newspaper reported the problems faced by plus-size women. Quoting from the book *Diary Of A Fat Housewife*, the author writes, "Dear Heavenly Father…Can't you see that my body is so fat that it causes me to suffer the pangs of hell…Why did you do this to me, Father?"[14] In her diary, the author was blaming God for her weight problem. Although she seems distraught, I have trouble buying into her reasoning that God was at fault for her over-eating. I have yet to experience God's hand force-feeding me potato chips!

The Bible tells us, **"A man's own folly ruins his life, yet his heart rages against the Lord." (Proverbs 19:3 NIV)** We blame everyone but ourselves—even God! Quite frankly, we are the primary source of most of our own problems. But we have trouble admitting that it is by our own hand that we do destructive things to ourselves and to others.

This blindness is removed when we take courage to face the truth about our actions. We are advised, **"If it is possible, as far as it depends on you, live at peace with everyone." (Romans 12:18 NIV)** This suggests that we have an active part in our relationships that we need to keep clear. Taking proper responsibility for our part breaks the habit of blame-shifting and helps us to grow in truth.

Specks and Planks

The second thinking pattern is the habit of reverse priority in our concern about sin. We become angry and upset about other people's sins while ignoring our own. Jesus illustrates our behavior this way: **"Why do you look at the speck of sawdust in your brother's eye and pay no attention to the plank in your own eye?…You hypocrite, first take the plank out of your own eye, and then you will see clearly to remove the speck from your brother's eye." (Matthew 7:3-5 NIV)** We reverse the priority in dealing with sin; it is more important to us to have another person's sin dealt with than to deal with our own.

We want God to change everyone else, and we will even jump in to help Him! I've heard women plead in prayer about their husbands, "Oh God, please make him more spiritual, more faithful, more

---

14   *The Plain Dealer*, Sept. 19, 1995

loving!" Yet we balk at the same discipline and scrutiny that would bring about change in us.

We also blindly think that we can change people. For instance, my friend Shirley spent a painful year trying to change her fiancee' into the man of God she felt he should be. Because he was in need of counseling, she drove him to seminars, made pastoral appointments for him, bought him books and tapes, and went to the altar with him for prayer. She thought she was preparing herself to be a godly, supportive wife, but after a year, there was still no change in him. A unison sigh of relief went up from family and friends when the engagement broke off.

"I can't do it anymore!" she sighed. "I can't change him. Only God can change a person!"

When we try to fix people, we attempt to correct how they think and behave. This reminds me of the time I changed the burnt out headlight in my car. To replace the bulb, I had to squeeze my hand between the light fixture and the car battery. There was only room for one hand; another hand from someone trying to help would have been in the way.

We do the same thing when we try to help God change a person's behavior. Too often we counsel people with advice we should be taking ourselves. Unless God gives us special insight to help someone see his problem, ours is the second hand that gets in the way. We need to give God His space to make the changes He wants. Our energies would be better spent hauling the planks out of our own life rather than interfering with the specks we find in others.

Self-Justification

The third pattern that blinds us from seeing clearly is self-justification. Once again we use our knowledge of good and evil to come up with good reasons for wrong actions, justifying everything we do. We twist the truth in our mind to find the right slant to answer our conscience. This way, we are able to right the wrong in our mind so that the wrong won't bother us. A companion to blame-shifting, we promptly defend ourselves while blaming others.

Our perceptions, ideas, notions, and opinions seem correct because they are so strong in our mind. **"All a man's ways seem right to him…" (Proverbs 21:2 NIV)** Our mind can be like a god to us. We have faith in what we think because our thoughts rise up from self. Our intelligence seems so strong that we don't even question it. Our thought life can become like a locked vault. Rather than unlock our reasoning with some interrogation, we carefully protect our point of view. We need to constantly check what we are thinking and believing if we are to come out of our blindness.

When Jesus comes into our life as Savior, He also sets up rule as King. To be ruled by a king is very foreign to us. Democracy allows for public opinion to become policy. American individuality is one reason why American Christians may not relate well to Jesus as King. In his book *Thy Kingship Come*, David Mains points out, "When reading the New Testament, we see Christ today filling many roles. He is our Savior, teacher, shepherd, healer, and so on. Because of our kingless culture, however, we tend to downplay this matter of keenly anticipated messiah or greatly anointed king."[15]

But our life in Christ is not a democracy. In Him, we are no longer free agents giving ourselves permission to live as we want. We need to adjust to the reality of having a personal King. That includes questioning our thought life and, if unacceptable to the King, change our mind!

Because Christ rules His kingdom from within the hearts of His subjects, the kingdom can only be experienced through a right relationship with the King. If we are justifying sin in our life, that will obstruct Christ's rule. That is why we are told to **"demolish arguments and every pretension that sets itself up against the knowledge of God, and we take every thought captive to make it obedient to Christ." (2 Corinthians 10:5 NIV)** This discipline of the mind opens our eyes to what we are doing so that we might see ourselves in light of the King.

---

15   Thy Kingship Come, p. 15

Will Someone Please Turn On The Lights?

God desires us to be free from sin's blindness so that we might be a people of vision. He wants us to clearly see His purposes. **"I tell you, open your eyes and look at the fields! They are ripe for harvest." (John 4:35 NIV)** We need to see ourselves as part of His eternal plan so that we will be compelled by that vision.

Paula Howard had a vision for the city of Cleveland to sponsor a float in the 1996 Rose Bowl parade, celebrating the city's bicentennial year. She mentioned it to her boss who brushed it off as a crazy idea. Five years later, he remembered her idea and asked if she had looked into it. She presented him with five years worth of notes and inquiry letters.

Working with some colleagues who caught the vision, the boss was able to win the support of the Mayor of Cleveland, the Governor of Ohio, and a substantial committee of business leaders. The concept was accepted by the Pasadena Tournament of Roses Association and Cleveland was represented in the parade. Because of one woman's vision, the daily paper boasted, "A half-billion people in 90 countries will know that there is a Cleveland, Ohio and what's happening here."[16]

How much more does God have His sights set on the world that people might know Him through Jesus Christ? But if God's people are stumbling around in blindness, remaining in their sin, how can He freely move? He needs people who will change their minds to dedicate themselves to His vision. We need to find our way out of the fog of falsehood. Then we can move forward with a singleness of purpose and vision to see the advancement of the kingdom as seen through the eyes of the King.

---

16   *The Plain Dealer*, Dec. 1995

PART II

DE-THRONE HER!

⁓ Chapter 6 ⁓
A CLOSER LOOK AT SELF

Anatural horror exists when a man (or woman) encounters a snake. One reference book introduced its study with this dialogue: "The snake: for most of us, it is a cold animal with slimy skin that slides towards its victim and injects it with mortal poison at lightening speed. Does any name in the animal world give rise to so many legends and fears, so much repulsion, terror or mortal fascination?"[17] That fear is certainly real for many people.

SNAKELIKENESS

After several years as a Christian, God asked me to look at a different kind of "snake." He wanted me to take a closer look at self. I was reading in the book of Jonah when God spoke these words to my mind, "Will you go into the belly of the whale to examine the guts of sin?" The Lord wanted to take me to see the depths of human sin and evil, including my own. During that time I was to write down everything I saw and eventually write this book. The Holy Spirit would be my Guide through those deep waters. The following is an explanation of what I saw.

Self is the part of us that resembles Satan—a mutant of the Old Serpent, his offspring well-preserved and living in the shadows. Man received the devil's nature when Adam rebelled against God and reached out to serve self. We do the same thing.

---

17   Snakes In Question, p. 10

John the Baptist spoke from this premise during his ministry of repentance. He called the people "snakes" as he saw the crowd approaching: **"You brood of vipers!" (Luke 3:7 NIV)** His insight hit home as thousands realized their vile, selfish nature and turned to God for forgiveness. The Lord's exposure of our "snakelikeness" is meant to repulse us enough to turn from our own selfish nature.

Let's go on to look at some of the characteristics of snakes and then moralize about human behavior. Perhaps we will be equally horrified as we encounter this snake.

OUR FOCUS

The unaware intruder will quickly discover that a snake is a touchy creature that requires wide range and a slow, careful step to escape its recourse of self-defense. In the same way, all of us have worked to enhance self by gathering ways, things or people to ourselves. Whatever we perceive to be ours we will vehemently protect. Like a "brood of vipers," people are quick to act out of self-preservation. The following three aspects of our nature cause us to guard self as we interact in the world with others.

The first aspect is our focus. We are primarily, if not exclusively, focused on ourselves and therefore selfish to the core. Selfishness is being too much concerned with one's own welfare or interests with little or no thought or care for others. When our minds are preoccupied with our own problems, there is minimal concern for others. We find other people's stories boring because are so intensely glued to watching the activities of self.

Scripture describes our singular focus this way: **"This is the exultant city that dwells securely, who says in her heart, 'I am and there is no one besides me.'" (Zephaniah 2:15 NAS)** Exultant means to rejoice greatly and find glory in. A city is a territory marked out by boundaries with powers of self-government. To dwell securely means to live in a safe, dependable place. With self, our "territory" is our life. We take pleasure in ruling our life and find comfort in its sure control. We also glory in ourselves, thinking, "I am it and there is no one else." Others may exist—but they don't matter. We are our most important concern. In our minds, we establish our rights and our rules, and then go on to protect our territory.

One of the key indicators of a life filled with self is touchiness. Because we are so convinced that everything revolves around us, we become angry when others don't conform to our demands. We are impatient at traffic lights or in waiting lines because we think that the world's activities should be at our command. We even grumble when the weather doesn't cooperate with our desires. How dare the sky not do what we say!

We are suspicious of other people's motives, often over-personalizing and reading offenses into their statements. "That person purposely did that against me!" we insist. We misinterpret the actions of others because we judge from the standpoint of self, but our reality is ill-defined.

Self is so alive to its own concerns that we turn against others. Our single focus "Me first!" outlook makes us to want to push others out of the way. We are cold towards others because we don't want them to have more than us. Just as cold-blooded snakes have a body temperature that adjusts to the surrounding air, land, or water, so do our circumstances influence our selfish moods. We may care-lessly vent our feelings of unhappiness on others when we are irri-tated. We have no regard for their feelings; we only care how we feel. "Cold-blooded" is our cultural term for murderers. It describes a person who is hardened, without pity, cruel, and insensitive. That is exactly the type of person we become when we constantly focus on self.

OUR DOMINATION

The second basic tendency is our domination. In our desire is to rule over others self behaves like a tyrant! This is the distorted result of man trying to make himself like God, even if it is only in his mind. Selfishness is this delusion lived out as people try to control their environment and enslave their fellow man.

One of our main attitudes is our expectation to be served by others. "Serve Me!" demands the selfish heart. An extreme example of this tendency is experienced by abuse victims. The book *Breaking The Cycle Of Abuse* describes this perverted lordship. "Batterers typically display extreme possessiveness and jealousy. These attitudes reflect his belief that his wife is a possession, something he owns and over which he must control. In extreme cases, he may demand that she remain at home, totally isolated from friends, neighbors and family members. He may actually lock her in the house and disconnect the phone to insure her imprisonment."[18]

We expect others to live to serve our needs. Man thinks he is great when he can dominate another person. Self seems to be glorified by its power to be lord. Even in friendships, people may use their strong personalities to assert themselves over someone else, establishing a master/slave relationship for their own benefit.

That is why Jesus had to correct his disciples' thinking by saying, **"You know that the rulers of the Gentiles lord it over them… Not so with you. Instead, whoever wants to become great among you must be your servant , and whoever wants to be first must be your slave—just as the Son of Man did not come to be served, but to serve, and to give his life as a ransom for many." (Matthew 20:25-28 NIV)** He did not want them to follow the natural inclinations of self and misuse their power. This teaching was a direct blow against the dominating efforts of self. By Jesus' example, greatness with God is using our lives to serve others rather than finding ways to make them serve us.

Using People

Many times we make friends with people because they are useful to us. This is the habit of using people. We are only interested in them for what they can do for us. Otherwise, we couldn't care less about them. As an illustration, in the cartoons we see the cat gazing at the rooster perched on the fence. Then we see the rooster through the cat's eyes—a steaming hot roast chicken served on a platter!

---

18   Breaking The Cycle of Abuse, p. 28

With similar motives, we may cultivate relationships on the basis of how helpful others might be to us. Instead of a true friendship, we are using others as a means of having our needs met. The Bible explains such expectations this way: **"For the prostitute reduces you to a loaf of bread, and the adulteress preys on your very life." (Proverbs 6:26 NIV)** In other words, selfish people feed off others by using them to get along in life.

King David's daughter, Tamar, was probably the saddest account in the Bible of someone being carelessly used by another person. Living in her father's household, she became the object of her half-brother Amnon's lust. **"Amnon became frustrated to the point of illness on account of his sister, Tamar, for she was a virgin, and it seemed impossible for him to do anything to her." (2 Samuel 13:2 NIV)** The strong feelings Amnon had were actually a love of himself as he imagined himself enjoying her beauty. He became sick at the thought of not having his desires met.

After scheming with a friend, Amnon tricked Tamar into fixing him a meal in his chambers. There, he forced himself on her while they were alone. He was not interested in being honorable towards her in marriage, nor did he think about how his actions would ruin her life. He was committed to satisfying himself by using her.

Afterwards, when self was served, his love turned into contempt for her. He was done with her and told her to get out. Selfishness can cause people to take complicated measures in manipulating others to serve them. We can misuse love through empty promises, flattery, false adulation, and seductive speech to set traps for people. All we really want is to use them for our benefit. When we are in the habit of using people, our confidence is in our ability to manipulate to get people to serve us rather than trusting God to meet our needs.

Irresponsibility

When we insist that others always do for us, we act like selfish babies. Irresponsibility dominates others by forcing them to do our work or fulfill our obligations because we won't. We demand that others take care of us. We shrug off our responsibilities and find ways to get others to wait on us. This attitude reminds me of a story a mother told about her nine month old son.

"We are going to have problems with this one," she sighed. "Everything that we are willing to do for him he will let us do. For example, he won't hold his bottle to feed himself—so we have to. And most babies arch their backs when they want to be picked up. But he just lays there and grunts. He just won't put forth the effort!"

When adults act this way, it could be described as the "Peter Pan Syndrome." In the story, Peter Pan makes a vow as a young boy. "I'll never grow up!" he says, because growing up is no fun. He doesn't want the responsibility of adulthood; he wants to stay and play. Living in "Never-Never Land" allows him to live out that vow.

We do the same thing when we inwardly refuse to make the transition from childhood to adulthood. We decide we don't ever want to grow up. At some point in our life, we may emotionally linger in an attitude of irresponsibility because we want to stay and play. We dwell in the childish land of self to make sure we are never ever giving and always, always taking. We may even think that our behavior is cute or that playing helpless is feminine. But these ploys are merely a result of stubbornness as we behave like selfish babies.

OUR WANTING

The third basic truth about self is how powerfully we want for ourselves. The selfish heart is bent on getting what it wants no matter what! Our hearts conjure up desires that can mislead us. **"The heart is deceitful above all things and beyond cure. Who can understand it?" (Jeremiah 17:9 NIV)** The tug from within can be extremely strong. So we need to look closely at what we crave for ourselves.

When I ride the bus to work in the morning I see people absorbed in their wanting. The ladies intensely flip through their mail-order catalogs, deciding on how to spend their money next. Like them, we say to ourselves, "Let me see. What will make my little heart happy?" Then we see something that seems like the answer and say, "Aha! That's perfect! I must have it!" Our wanting can become a ravenous appetite within us.

King David's wandering eyes and wanting heart were the cause of his downfall with Bathsheba. Restless one night, bored, and at general ease, David wanted some new excitement in his life. **"One evening David got up from his bed and walked around the roof of the palace. From the roof he saw a woman bathing. The woman was very beautiful, and David sent someone to find out about her. The man said, 'Isn't this Bathsheba, the daughter of Eliam and the wife of Uriah the Hittite?' Then David sent messengers to get her. She came to him, and he slept with her." (2 Samuel 11:2-3 NIV)**

Just like David, we defy sound reasoning when self wants. Our cravings can make us temporarily crazy as we lust for the things we see. In Jim Bakker's book, *I Was Wrong*, he describes the restlessness he felt at the time of his affair with Jessica Hahn. He wanted to be a success in ministry, he wanted to make Tammy Faye jealous in their marriage and, for the moment, he wanted to be wanted.[19]

At weak times like these (and we all have them) our thinking stops as our wanting takes over. It draws us with magnetic force to what we think we need, taking us places we shouldn't go, having relationships we shouldn't have, doing things we know we shouldn't do. The difficulties we get into are the reason why we need to surrender our desires to Christ. His rule will hold us back from acting upon our selfish wanting and harming ourselves.

Fantasy

When we set our heart on something, we won't budge until we get it. Sometimes we set our hearts on things and practically make ourselves sick with wanting them. The source of our extreme wanting is our own imagination. We imagine a certain outcome and then set our will to see it come true.

The Serpent beguiled Eve into imagining what she could have for herself. Her mind became a playground where her fantasies could

---

19   I Was Wrong, p. 12

be lived out. As she lingered on his deception, she was no longer in touch with reality. Instead, she took a brief trip into the exciting land of possibilities where she could see herself as the central figure.

In the same way, we have the ability to escape into fantasy with our minds, living in the comfort of a false reality that we create. There we may pretend to be someone else or that others are the way we want them to be. Our melancholy moods may cause us to pine away, living in the land of "If Only," wishing our lives away.

I'll never forget the woman who wanted me to sew for her when I was working as a seamstress in college. We met at a fabric store and she explained that she wanted to have a special gown to wear to a relative's wedding. She became very emotional as she told how she needed to prove her adequacy to her in-laws. If only she could show up at the wedding as an indescribable beauty, then the family would be so astonished that they would be ashamed of the way they had treated her all these years and apologize!

She dashed over to the sheer fabrics and started to unravel a bolt of powder blue chiffon. For about a half hour I watched her waltz between the aisles, draping herself with different colors of material. I suggested that she call me after she decided what she wanted, but she never did.

I felt sorry for her. It seemed so obvious with her stocky, mid-40's figure that her fantasy was not possible. Yet she had played out the scene so much in her mind that the image had become real to her. She didn't realize how she was acting in the store because she was so lost in her fantasy.

Christ doesn't want us wandering around in our minds, lost in fantasy. He wants us to stay in touch with Him so that we can distinguish the truth from the imaginary. Living out false images of ourselves may seem like a safe plan of escape from the pains of life, but God prefers to cushion our blows with Himself.

Romance

One of the strongest pulls on the hearts of women is their desire for romantic love. When we picture in our minds how we want a man to focus all of his attention on us, constantly lavishing us with his affections, then we live with false expectations of human love. Women who live for romance are taken captive by their emotions and live in a dream world.

One woman explained to me that if she couldn't have romance then she felt her life wasn't worth living. Although she was a Christian, she was busy in her heart seeking romance, wanting a man to live just for her, rather than seeking God. The problem comes when God does not fill our lives with careless, giddy romance. We can become angry with disappointment when He does not fulfill our vision of love.

This happened to a woman I met at a singles gathering. Guests had been asked to bring picture albums of their vacation trips and to share their adventures with others. This woman showed us pictures of her trip to Paris, France. She said she wanted to go to Paris because it was the most romantic city in the world. In other words, if she was to ever find romance, it would be found there.

One weekend, the tour group took an evening boat ride through the heart of the city on the Seine River. The view was breathtaking. A seventy-year old tour guide saw her sitting along, pining away and felt sorry for her, so he sat with her. This only made her feel worse!

Her trip had been such a disappointment that her faith in God had been shaken. She closed the book and retreated to the couch; she had fully expected God to fulfill her dreams of romantic love in Paris.

We should not limit God's love by insisting it take the form of romance. God is love, and we need to let Him reveal Himself as He pleases. The great ending to this story was that God moved her to another church and she met the man she married!

RESPONSIBILITY

Responsibility is God's antidote for selfishness. It forces us to forget about ourselves in order to look out for the needs of others. We must think about others to be able to take proper care of them.

Accepting responsibility means extra work that puts a strain on our mind and emotions. In that very exercise is the benefit to us. We must tap into our Resource to fulfill our obligations. Christ's equipping follows the burden we have agreed to carry. Our meetings with Christ to receive His guidance will enable us to grow in stature to perform our duties

For example, even as a Christian, a single friend of mine admitted to living a totally selfish life. She was in misery as God reminded her daily about her sin. Finally, she surrendered her rights to her life. She agreed to take on a degree of responsibility by serving in her church. Now she helps lead a thriving inner-city youth group and has matured in her Christian walk. She grew as a result of the demanding responsibility she had in teaching needy teenagers.

It is clearly God's will for people to leave their childhood and grow up. He wants us to live responsibly towards Him and towards others. God wants to raise us up to be adults who are dependable, capable of making godly decisions, and mature in our faith. **"Then we will no longer be infants, tossed back and forth by waves... Instead...we will in all things grow up into him who is the Head, that is Christ." (Ephesians 4:14-15 NIV)** Taking on responsibility as God directs will transform our selfish nature into the nature of Christ the Good Shepherd and Christ the Loving Servant.

LOVING OTHERS AS OURSELVES

The greatest responsibility that we are given in Christ is to emulate Christ in His love for others. **"This is how we know what love is: Jesus Christ laid down his life for us. And we ought to lay down our lives for our brothers." (1 John 3:16 NIV)** If we remain in selfishness, that is a sign that we are resisting the true meaning of Christianity. God gave Himself in love, but we won't.

True brotherly love means putting off self as first and foremost in order to regard others first. Love for others checks and then changes our aggressive, self-absorbed behavior. Unselfish love requires a radical change of mind followed by a deliberate change in our actions. Brotherly love motivates us to do for others without expecting anything in return. It is an innocent and pure deed done to honor Christ. Love for others is a reflection of Christ's supremacy because it is an outward sign of how dear we hold Him in our hearts.

Small acts of kindness, thoughtfulness, and compassion are simple ways that Christians can evidence the divine nature within them. In Christ, we are given the ability to show respect, to be grateful, to encourage, to be courteous, and to give praise. All of these ways impart life to others, building them up as God intends. God wants us to practice doing good until it becomes natural for us to do so. Loving kindness becomes a part of who we are.

Scripture speaks of putting childish ways behind, referring to the basic aspects of our focus, our domination, and our selfish wanting. When we put off selfishness, we can, by faith, give ourselves in love. As self nature is shed, these three things remain, **"faith, hope and love. But the greatest of these is love." (1 Corinthians 13:3 NIV)**

∾ Chapter 7 ∾
PRIDE

The snake uses intimidation tactics to protect itself from its predators. It rises up on its spine or swells itself, making it appear larger than it really is. This protective instinct of the snake pictures the work of pride in our lives. Pride swells us to make us seem greater, more intelligent, more powerful or more important than we really are.

In our sin, we hold an inward false impression that we are like gods and as a result we tend to believe that we are invincible. Conceit is a trick that we play in our minds, fooling ourselves into thinking that we are great. We try to impress others to further validate our mental self image. The prideful person swells in his attitudes about himself, yet does not know that it distances him from God. **"Knowledge puffs us, but love builds up. The man who thinks he knows something does not yet know as he ought to know." (1 Corinthians 8:1-2 NIV)**

SELF-GLORY
In pagan cultures, the snake is often worshipped as a god, highly regarded as a powerful life-force that grants fertility and immortality.[20] Rejecting the knowledge of the Creator, man falls into worshipping the creature, creating gods as an explanation for human ability and harmony in nature. We may not worship snakes in our culture, but we fall into the same creature worship when we worship

---

20   Snakes In Question, p. 126

ourselves. Pride comes from sinful reasoning that glories in self, crediting self as the source of our abilities.

Originally in Heaven all eyes gazed upon God. He was the center of all worship; every heavenly being looked at Him and voiced their admiration. God was exalted and adored for the love, beauty, wisdom, power, and glory that radiated from Him. **"You are worthy, our Lord and God, to receive glory and honor and power, for you created all things and by your will they were created and have their being." (Revelation 4:11 NIV)** God was seen as the undeniable source of all life, substance, and being for all things.

Tragically, Lucifer lowered his eyes to become fascinated with his own self. He saw that he was exquisite and vain reasoning made him imagine that he was the source of all he was. **"Your heart became proud on account of your beauty and you corrupted your wisdom because of your splendor." (Ezekiel 28:17 NIV)**

By nature, man was infected with this same false reasoning of self-worship and pride. We were also created as magnificent creatures. But as we adore self, our personalities become filled with lofty attitudes such as conceit, arrogance, self-satisfaction, and self-importance. When we glory in self, we will not easily see our attitudes as sinful.

I WAS WRONG

One serious result of pride is our inability to admit we are wrong. It just kills some of us to say, "I'm sorry. I was wrong." Our pride won't even let the words form in our mouth, much less take hold in our heart. We become so hardened with pride that we refuse to betray self, even when the truth is obvious.

Pride will also make us want to prove ourselves right in disagreements. That is why the Bible warns, **"Pride only breeds quarrels." (Proverbs 13:10 NIV)** Both sides try to defend themselves to prove themselves right. We muster the energy to justify ourselves to keep our reputation intact. This defense mechanism is probably the greatest block to the work of repentance. We not only won't admit we were wrong, we also feel the need to prove we were right.

WILL POWER

One of the most common works of pride in our American culture is will power that ascribes personal power to self. Americans are proud of their achievements which result from selfish ambition. We use aggression and human force to get through life, and feel tremendously powerful about it. Management levels in the workplace are breeding grounds for those who choose to explore their will power.

Of course, the pride of will power is found at every level. I was in K-Mart one evening and stepped into a check-out lane that was clear. The cashier was a cute, sandy-haired twenty-year old who was yawning and glancing at her watch, wanting to go home. I smiled and suggested that maybe the night would go fast. She responded by making a quick gesture of horns on her head, jerking her head forward, lowering her voice and saying, "I will it so!"

As shocking as this sounds, this is the spirit of this age convincing people that they have personal power, that what they say will become so. People exalt themselves in their own minds so much that they believe they are their own power source.

COMPETITION

Another earmark of pride is the way people work against each other in competition. There is a saying that "love makes the world go 'round." But King Solomon looked at men and saw that competition was actually the driving force behind man's activity. **"And I saw that all labor and all achievement spring up from man's envy of his neighbor." (Ecclesiastes 4:4 NIV)** Man keeps a watchful eye on what his neighbor is doing, and then sets himself to out-do him. We see life as a big game and aggressively play to win.

The main problem with competition is that it has a teeter-totter effect on relationships. For us to feel the high of being on top, someone else must ride at ground level to give us something to compare to. Envious comparison of others perverts our motives to want to get ahead.

The Apostle Paul warns the church not to be caught up in spiritual pride and competition because it wreaks havoc on unity.

63

Disunity stifles the work of God from being done. **"Do not go beyond what is written. Then you will not take pride in one man over against another being done." (1 Corinthians 4:6 NIV)** In trying to impress others with their spirituality, people were complicating the simplicity of the faith. Notice the words "over against" which proves that any attempt to out-do will also undo. Competition is people jeering each other on, while cooperation is people cheering each other on.

COOPERATION

If Christians enjoy winning anything, it should be winning victories against a common enemy. There is nothing more satisfying than working together to see relief come from answered prayer. I remember a time when my friend Debbie and I were helping a young family whose children were being horribly afflicted by the enemy.

Without planning, Debbie was led by the Lord to stay up all Friday night to fast and pray. At 6:00 a.m. Saturday, God woke me up and led me to fast and pray throughout the day as I did my chores. Later when we compared notes, my wake-up call was the exact time God signaled Debbie to lie down and get some rest.

As a result, the devil could not stand against this simple orchestration of unity and obedience. The back-to-back prayer formed a wedge that drove him out, leaving those children healed and in peace. The key was that we were not trying to impress each other, but instead enjoyed the wonder of the leading of the Holy Spirit. Debbie and I have sweet memories of that victory as we have learned to cooperate with God and with each other.

We must understand our need to work together as Christians, yet we can lay no claim to the spiritual work being done. The finished goal does not point to "Me" or "You" but involves "us" and points to Christ. This was Paul's thought when he wrote, **"I planted the seed, Apollos watered it, but God made it grow. So neither**

he who plants nor he who waters is anything, but only God, who makes things grow." (1 Corinthians 3:6-7 NIV)

If we set aside personal ambition, achievement, and competition to learn to accept another person's part in ministry, then God's work will not be hindered by self-glory, power plays, and human pride.

~ Chapter 8 ~
ANGER

While attending a family reunion in North Carolina, one morning I went for a walk in an open, grassy field. Carefully, I watched where I stepped because I knew that snakes in the South are dangerous. Snakes, in general, are not safe animals because they strike out and bite without much provocation.

People who are angry are not safe to be near, either. In their anger, they lash out at others, using angry reactions to let people know they are hurting, fearful, or just unhappy. We instinctively know that anger carries a degree of power, so we inflict pain on others by using cutting words and human force. We strike out at others in a way that is felt but not seen.

When we become upset about something, we can feel emotional energy rising within us. This sensation of adrenaline should not be mistaken for God's power. Fury and rage are acts of the flesh. Stored up anger from unresolved conflict may feel powerful, but should not be used as a source of strength nor a way to bring about change. The Bible says, **"Man's anger does not bring about the righteous life that God desires." (James 1:20 NIV)** If we are depending on our anger to get us through difficult situations then we are not living the right life that God wants.

ANGER AS A TOOL

God showed me that when people use anger to empower themselves, it is like a man carrying around a hammer. When something upsets him, he just hammers at the situation by showing his anger until he is satisfied. I see this often when people are unhappy about a problem. They slam doors, yell at others, and throw a fit. Anger is their dependable tool to express their disagreement. No one can get near them to reason with them until their anger subsides.

Anger was the tool that Cain used when he killed his brother Abel. God rejected Cain's grain offering and used that blocked goal to get his attention. God was more concerned about the seeds He saw growing in Cain's heart. **"Then the Lord said to Cain, 'Why are you angry...if you do what is right, will you not be accepted?'" (Genesis 4:6 NIV)**

But Cain had already decided how to solve his problem of rejection. "No thanks," he thought, "I'll handle this myself." Cain refused to submit to God, allowing anger to become the ruling force in his life. He turned and served his new god by slaying his brother. When we habitually turn to anger as a way of solving our problems, then we obey and serve anger as our god. The foothold that the devil wants is to make us automatically turn to anger as our solution instead of Christ.

VENTING

Often times we vent our angry feelings through screaming, yelling, sarcasm, glaring facial expressions, or sharp words. When directed at others, they all bring a degree of pain that is self-serving and wrong. Our sharp tongue can become like a whip that is used to scold, berate, or otherwise convey our angry dissatisfaction. Rather than defend our right to vent, we need to see our anger as sin. **"The acts of the sinful nature are obvious...hatred, discord, jealousy, fits of rage..." (Galatians 5:20 NIV)**

This use of anger could be described as the "Little Red Riding Hood Syndrome." Here comes Little Red skipping along with her goody basket on her way to Granny's, singing as she goes.

"I'm so nice. I'm so wonderful because of all I do-be-do-be-do!" Then, suddenly a boulder rolls across her path blocking her way and she sees no way around it.

"This trip was supposed to be easy!" she mutters. At that point she decides to let everyone in the forest know that she is unhappy. She whips off her red cover-up and, lo and behold, becomes the Big Bad Wolf!

Now operating in a different mode, she draws strength from her anger, and huffs and puffs and blows the forest down! Satisfied with her newly leveled path and her ability to intimidate forest-dwellers, she skips merrily on to Granny's!

In real life, there is nothing comical about leveling our paths with anger. We need to stop and take a serious look if we find ourselves re-enacting this scene. We may feel better after we vent, but most likely we have unleashed a destructive force in our relationships. Our repressed anger causes tension for others because they are waiting for us to blow. Friends and family will stop taking the risk of getting close to us after too many incidents of our venting.

God does not approve of man's industry negatively motivated by anger. **"Better…a man who controls his temper than one who takes a city." (Proverbs 16:32 NIV)** I have read articles that suggest that people should channel their anger into something good. This advice only offers a sugar coating for wrong behavior. A friend of mine thought she could channel her anger into physical exercise. When she got mad, she would go to the gym and siphon off her adrenaline doing aerobics. Her anger would subside for a time, but it would surface again during the next difficulty. God does not condone recycling anger to get things done nor does He approve of the results we seem to get from our venting. We are much better off to learn self-control.

POLITE ANGER

Women seem to have a way of masking their anger to maintain an appearance of innocence. They can be very aggressive in relationships, and yet smile and keep their composure. Women are also experts at being indirect, supposedly not wanting to hurt people's feelings by speaking directly. And yet this same side door approach is exactly what we use to get our digs in. To clarify this, let me explain the "Five P's of Polite Anger":

Punishing: We use this subtle retaliation method against those who offend us or disagree with us. We determine a punishment we feel they deserve and then carry it out. These ways include withdrawing from the relationship, openly embarrassing a person with ridicule, and using sarcasm. We never forget an offense, we just lie in wait, watching for an opportunity to take revenge. We give the silent treatment to non-verbally communicate our anger rather than discuss the problem openly. Punishing also includes expressions like "I told you so!" or martyr-like comments such as, "Never mind, I'll do it myself!"

Pouting: This attitude comes from self-pity and blame shifting. We take punishing a step further by putting on a false sadness that insinuates victimization. We picture ourselves as poor, innocent victims, and then retreat into our unhappiness with unrealistic measures of blame. Moodiness, worked-up tears, and stomping out of the room are special effects that accentuate pouting.

Pretending: This behavior keeps our opponent guessing while we silently nurse our anger. When someone wants to talk honestly about a problem, we say "There is nothing wrong!" or "I'm not mad!" Maintaining a facade of being nice is more important to us than admitting that we have some anger issues to resolve. We don't want anyone to see that we are angry, so we lie about it.

Pettiness: We may protect our anger because we want to feel the strength from it. We don't want to give up the force from our aggression. So we shift the focus of our anger onto non-issues rather than discuss the real issue and get over it. Pettiness creates a smoke-screen whereby we pretend to be offended by a molehill rather than address the mountain that is really bothering us. This way, we throw people off track and keep our anger. "I'm angry about the way you planted the petunias!" we claim, while the real problem goes untouched. We use pettiness as a cover-up because we prefer to keep the sin.

Proving: With this attitude we say to ourselves, "I'll show them!" Using anger, we find the energy for college education, sports awards, business promotions, and other accomplishments done to prove our offender wrong. This anger is rooted in people-pleasing. We have suffered rejection and we are angry about it. Our offender may have long forgotten his or her callous remarks about our worth, but we are still fueled by someone's opinion and work to perform in a way that will surely speak up for us. Sadly, by the time we reach our goals, circumstances change, and the offender may move or pass away, and will never be able to acknowledge our efforts. Our furious energy proves nothing.

Polite anger may help us to keep a facade of innocence, but God sees the anger that we are holding against others. We will only experience relief from this wrong energy when we confess it to God as sin.

PEACE

A lifetime of pent-up anger robs us of any peace. As Christians, the Bible says that God has called us to live in peace. **"Let the peace of Christ rule in your hearts, since as members of one body you were called to peace…" (Colossians 3:15 NIV)** This describes the inner tranquillity that is possible when we forsake anger as our god. Rather than turn to anger out of habit, we should turn to Christ to solve our problems and soothe our fears.

This trust is based on the fact that our peace with God was secured by Christ. He made peace for us. **"Therefore, since we have been justified through faith we have peace with God through our Lord Jesus Christ…" (Romans 5:1 NIV)** Christ did not retaliate when He arose from being brutally murdered on the cross. Jesus refrained from anger and, instead, offered a peaceful way to unite us with God. His mind was set on peace and so should ours.

Because all human offenses have stricken Christ, we have no right to keep personal offenses alive through anger. Anger is but a foothold for the misery of the devil. We need to look at how we are destroying peace in our relationships. The following is a poem that might help us face the truth about our anger.

Angry Heart

Angry heart,
Who can love you?
You shun the approach
Of love drawing near.

Angry heart,
Who can reach you?
Buried in blame
From everyone's fault.

Angry heart,
Who can bear you?
You scorch the hand
Like a fiery hot coal.

Angry heart,
Who can heal you?
No earthly cure
For your hidden sores.

Angry heart,
Who can tell you?
Only the One
Who speaks from within.

The truth is that deep anger issues make us unbearable to live with and ruin our peace. Christ can and will bring inner resolve if we just let Him reason with our angry heart.

∾ Chapter 9 ∾
HATRED

If anger is the bite of the snake, then hatred is the poison that flows from its fangs into its victim. Biting hurts, but poison in the bloodstream kills. Hatred, then, is a powerful sense of ill-will against others, even to the extent of wishing them dead. We may not see ourselves as being capable of these strong feelings, but the Bible says this is common practice among us. **"We lived in malice and envy, being hated and hating one another." (Titus 3:3 NIV)** In our natural state, we hate people—not sin. Because God has shown us His kindness and mercy through Christ, He expects us to hate sin—not people. For that change to take place, we will need to understand what fosters hatred in us.

Hatred is a product of self that comes from a general perception of people as intruders upon our closely guarded life. When someone oversteps his boundaries, we work up resentment against him. Hating is our way of coping with the intrusion and is used as a weapon to satisfy our urge for retaliation. The strong ill-will we feel fools us into believing that we have done something to cure the situation.

Hating also results when intruders genuinely hurt us, but we do not turn the offense over to God. As we hold it in, the hurting grows into hating. We carry this within us, just as the snake's poison glands are concealed and carried within its own body.

CONTEMPT

There are several types of hatred that may surface in our relationships. One kind is contempt which is a subtle, haughty, "look down your nose" hatred towards those we deem below us. Our feelings of superiority result in despising others. We express contempt when we refer to others as being "idiots!"

If we have been especially fortunate to have intelligence, good looks, or financial success, we may be tempted to breathe it all in and say, "Hey, look at me!" Even if we have just one area in which we feel superior, we use that to anchor our security, and look down on others in contempt.

In our success oriented culture, we are especially hateful towards broken people. We regard brokenness as a negative and become impatient when people don't "have it together." Perhaps we do not understand God's use of the meek and lowly, nor do we respect His Spirit upon them.

One morning on my way to work I dropped some money into the outstretched Styrofoam cup of a street beggar. I heard a soft voice say, "God bless you!" Looking closer, I saw a woman about my age, her tiny body leaning on crutches against the stone building like a nesting sparrow.

As I spoke to her about Jesus, she brightened up.

"Oh, I'm a born-again believer!" she assured me. "I tried to do things on my own strength, but that doesn't work. So I depend on Him for everything!"

I was surprised to find her to be a sister in the Lord, more valuable than a thousand sparrows. The thought ricocheted in my mind that this could have easily been me. That same haunting reminder, I believe, is what we hate most about broken people. We don't want their situation to, somehow, rub off onto us. Being near them immediately puts us in touch with how much we have, followed by a nagging moral responsibility to share. We feel the tug, so we distance ourselves with contempt because we don't want anything to be taken away from us.

I don't know why the Lord allows this degree of brokenness, but I do know His thoughts towards those like her. **"Though the Lord is on high, he looks upon the lowly." (Psalm 138:6 NIV)** He does not look down upon the lowly with contempt like we do, but instead regards them in love.

ENVY

The opposite end of the scale from contempt is envy. Due to feelings of inferiority, we harbor selfish ill-will against those who seem to have an advantage over us. This attitude grows out of false assumptions of what we feel we deserve to have. When we don't have something and see someone else having it, we covetously hate them for it for what they possess.

When we give in to our insecurities, we ruin friendships with divisions that begin in our heart. **"For where you have envy and selfish ambition, there you find disorder and evil practice." (James 3:16 NIV)** This can be especially poisonous among Christians who glare at others who seem to be enjoying a degree of prosperity, either personally or in ministry. We let our eyes wander off of Christ and allow our emotions to want.

Our resentment is the failing grade in God's test of our belief in His goodness. **"I am still confident of this: I will see the goodness of the Lord in the land of the living." (Psalm 27:13 NIV)** Whether we immediately see His goodness or not, God is still good. We need to discipline ourselves to be content with what He has given us and stop comparing with others. Be glad for God's goodness in whatever manner He has given.

SELF-HATRED

Part of the problem of envy may be rooted in self-hatred. Self-hatred is a measure of resentment against our own selves for what we feel we lack. If we have believed the enemy's lies pointing out our faults, comparing us to everyone else, then we may view ourselves as being worthless.

Holding hard feelings against ourselves results in a type of self-punishment. We think, "If I inflict pain on myself for being such a horrible person, then I will get the punishment I deserve!" Consequently, we berate or purposely neglect ourselves out of self-hatred. This self-inflicted suffering may even seem "Christian" as we flail ourselves with criticism. There is a reverse pride can that accompany our insecurities. We try to boost ourselves with pride rather than face our insecurities and self-hatred.

We need not punish ourselves with self-hatred. Christ's death on the cross on our behalf fulfills God's requirement for justice. God will accept us if we admit sin and receive His pardon for what we've done. We should not attempt to add anything to that finished work because we can't.

Our pardon was undeserved, true enough, but no less available to us. Perhaps we have yet to grasp how someone could love us in spite of who we are. We need to fully accept and become comfortable with that truth. To resist self-hatred, we need to believe in the One who loves us rather than accepting the lies from the one who hates us.

MAN-HATING

One of the most popular forms of hatred that women in our society indulge in is man-hating. The Feminist Movement used man-hating as one of its most powerful uniting factors. With man as the common enemy, the movement mustered its strength through a "Yea for our team! Boo for your team!" mentality. Now it seems that women today don't love men anymore. Instead they love to hate men!

One time I worked in an office managed by an angry divorcee. Balanced on top of her PC tube was a "Gumby" doll that looked like a man dressed in business clothes. Throughout the day we would pass her desk and see the doll mangled into all sorts of physically impossible positions. The other women in the office thought this display of temper was hilarious.

76

Another woman I worked with once made a comment about her preferences in dating. "I like the kind of guy I can knock around!" she remarked. This attitude is so widespread that it has become marketable. Recently, a friend described a T-shirt being sold at a mall entitled "The Perfect Man." It showed a picture of an iced gingerbread man. The caption read, "He's sweet. He's quiet. And if he annoys you—just bite his head off!"

This prevailing animosity in our culture has filtered into the Church. We have given in to the temptation to lay blame on men in general. In our women's groups we casually remark, "All men are _____!" Then we fill in the blank with all sorts of hateful descriptions. One Sunday in a church restroom I heard a woman complaining about the placement of the mirrors. "That's because it was designed by a man!" she explained sourly.

God showed me that when sisters feed on this attitude it resembles swine at a feeding trough. We munch and munch, making a meal out of malice, and then wave others to join us for a snack. Man-hating is another way we use our knowledge of evil to help soothe our offenses. Forbidden fruit has now decomposed into leftovers at the trough. How many times will "Eve" allow herself to be deceived?

As women, we have probably all had times when we felt offended, misunderstood, or neglected by men. But that is no reason to let our hurting turn into poisonous hating. Many times we blame men for holding us back from gaining success. To a greater degree, I believe we hold ourselves back with our own fears and disobedience.

Rather than be disgruntled, we need to ask God to show us a glimpse of His supreme plan for us. The overall good God has in mind can actually be overwhelming! Dwelling in Christ in a very roomy place. **"You have…set my feet in a spacious place." (Psalm 31:8 NIV)** We can feel good about the important work God has for women. In Christ, there is lots of room to learn and grow, to serve, and discover our eternal value. But we won't go anywhere without first releasing others from angry blame.

77

THE AMBASSADOR

I have been very fortunate to be healed of my own warped view of men by enjoying true Christian brotherhood. My friendship with Kevin thrives on the essential ingredient of mutual respect. At first, I was concerned about becoming close friends with a man who, I didn't believe, was the one for me to marry. So I asked God, "Is this right?" The Lord showed me that He approved of the purity of the relationship because "It stops the war!" Male and female getting along well, appreciating the differences, building each other up—it stops the war.

One time during a phone conversation with Kevin I began to voice my strong convictions about God. I caught myself getting too preachy and climbed down from my "soap box."

"So much for my two cents," I said as a disclaimer.

"You keep it up with your two cents," he assured me, "because some day it will add up to wealth in eternity."

I enjoy my freedom to be at ease with Kevin because he has never crushed my feelings. His deep security in his own position with Christ anchors him to lift up, not put down. Like a brother, he looks out for me and gives me strong advice from a different perspective.

Another time he showed me a picture of himself taken at a New Year's Eve party. He wore a dark suit with a bow tie and a red cummerbund. I thought to myself, "He looks like an ambassador in this picture." An ambassador is a representative from a foreign country who is chosen for his diplomacy and ability to make peace. For this purpose, he is sent to where there may be hostility between two nations. The ambassador willingly crosses the border and extends good will to establish smooth relations.

In all fairness, haven't we all had male ambassadors extend themselves at some point with help and kindness? Maybe a door was opened for us when our hands were full of kids and groceries. Or an unexpected word of praise or encouragement was voiced when we really needed to hear something good said to us. Stop to consider all the godly ambassadors on Christian television, radio, or in the pulpit whom we can respect and learn from.

Are we willing to give up our ill-will when someone crosses our boundaries to show us good will? That is what Christ did. He crossed the border from divinity to humanity to be the supreme Ambassador sent from God, and His kindness is endless.

Our self-satisfaction in paying back harm for hurt is not worth it. Life is too short to spend our energies hating. These inner poison glands must be lanced! Through Christ, we can make a deliberate effort to stop the war within ourselves and with others. Then, with the poison gone, there will be more room in our lives to receive the expressions of good will that God intends for us.

∽ Chapter 10 ∽
FEAR

Sometimes the snake does not use aggression against its ene-
mies but, instead, hides itself among the leaves or coils around
itself, tucking its head under its own body for protection. The snake
is responding to its natural instinct of fear.

Likewise, fear causes people to dread an assumed harmful outcome as if it were real. They respond to fear by finding ways to avoid
what they think might happen. The power of fear seizes the heart,
halting activity because of irrational beliefs. Simple tasks may seem
enormous when fear overwhelms us.

For example, a young mother in a beginner writing class showed
early promise in writing children's stories. Classmates asked her if
she wanted to try to have her work published, but she refused. She
was worried that if she sent an inquiry letter, she might mis-fold the
paper for the envelope. She thought that if the publisher opened
the letter and saw the uneven folds, he would think she was stupid and reject her stories. She reasoned that the possibility of being
published was not worth the risk of being thought of as stupid. As
unusual as this may sound, the anticipated outcome she had pictured in her mind was very real to her. The fear had a strong enough
grip to stop her from exploring her talent.

From this instance, we can see that the devil paints circumstances in our minds with one color of paint—pitch black. Normally, he needs only one coat if we believe what he has told us
and we see the situation from his point of view. Irrational fear also

makes us over-react to our problems. We may flip out over relatively simple matters because we assume that there is no possible solution. Yet we have not factored God into the picture. With Him, we can calm ourselves down enough to think clearly about our options and expect Him to reveal an answer. **"So do not fear, for I am with you." (Isaiah 41:10 NIV)**

INSECURITY

Insecurity is the painful, overly-sensitive, hyper-awareness of the insufficiency of self. It is the assurance that the devil gives us that we are unloved, have no value, and can't do anything right. The enemy adds extra pressure by pointing out that everyone else has a measure of what we feel we are missing. Our feelings of exclusivity compel us to inwardly hide out for fear someone will find out about our shortcomings and failures.

This intense personal fear is a real battleground for many women. To be freed from our hiding places, we must realize that our victory can only be won inwardly. We cannot overcome our insecurities by outward means. Beauty makeovers, expensive clothes, jewelry, or huge homes cannot compensate for feelings of inadequacy. Modern day "Dress for Success" theories may seem to offer an answer, but in truth, do nothing to touch the inner self cowering in fear. These efforts just boost the pride even further, and we do not need to be dressed in that kind of power.

Insecurity also is not cured by clinging to other people, like a security blanket. Forcing others to hover over us to make sure we feel safe in unsure situations will only shackle them with our need. For instance, at a retreat for youth leaders, attendees were divided into small groups for a time of discussion. One of the leaders kept looking nervously over at his wife who was in a different group. Before they left home, she had made him promise to stay by her side the whole weekend. Her insecurities had worked her into a panic about the possibility of facing a crowd of strangers alone. This couple's preoccupation with fear now robbed them of the training and spiritual enrichment they needed for leadership.

Our insecurities need to be seen as fear that we are obeying. God will certainly not condemn us for what we lack. He is sure of His sufficiency for us and is able to impart the revelation of Himself that we need. He is more than willing to build us up to have healthy personalities. In fact, He takes pleasure in bringing us out of our hiding places, but we must be willing to come out.

CONTROL

Many women refuse to challenge themselves, preferring instead to settle into familiar patterns of living which they can control. The cause of their mediocrity is fear of change. When we shut ourselves off from new experiences, then life winds down to a predictable repetition of sameness. Control is our attempt to monitor sameness.

We may do this because we know that change forces us to make personal adjustments. The way we are and how we live is called into question. To avoid that, we would rather have a predictable Christ who will not disturb our well-controlled lifestyle. With a routine we can count on, we guard its permanence by saying, "We always do things this way!"

But change is a given for the Christian. We automatically become involved in the process of change when we step foot into God's kingdom. To be "transformed" means to change the form, nature, character, or disposition of something. We can almost hear the wheels turning and the gears grinding in the following verse as God plans out His change in us. **"And we eagerly await a Savior from there, the Lord Jesus Christ, who by the power that enables him to bring everything under his control, will transform..." (Philippians 3:20-21 NIV)** A Christian should be open and willing to change. Any change initiated by God is meant to take us to a new level of Christ's supremacy in our life.

CONTROLLING OTHERS

People also react to fear by exerting control over others. We decide what others should think, say, and do, and then take action to make them do what we want. When we control, we make up personal rules that we expect others to follow. Control is the communication of our expectations and demands on others. For example, one woman in the church decided that she needed a mother figure in her life, so she made it a habit of approaching women leaders with needy, baby-ish behavior. Persistence in this way made her very controlling. If the women did not comply with her expectations, she felt rejected, offended, and upset that her relational rules had not been followed.

The success we gain in controlling others quickly turns into bossy-ness. We find that it is easier and safer to sit and bark orders to others rather than doing things for ourselves. We learn to play "god" by telling others what to do and insisting they do it. Somehow, we see ourselves as ruling the world from the couch while safely snuggled up in an afghan. Imagine that!

God showed me that a person who is trying to control is like a child playing the game of "Freeze Tag." For the person who is "It", the goal is to "freeze" the other players by tagging them. According to the rules, when they are "frozen" they are not allowed to move. The one who is "It" must constantly guard those who are "frozen" to keep them that way and "re-freeze" those who have been released by a free opponent.

When we control, we become overly involved in ruling life. We try to keep things "frozen" and familiar. Then time slips away and all we've done is spend our lives keeping things the same. **"The man who loves his life will lose it, while the man who hates his life in this world will keep it for eternal life." (John 12:25 NIV)** When we never risk what is familiar, we miss out on the glory of maturity through growth. If we would only learn to let go, Christ will surely fill us with the wonder, excitement, and amazement of Himself.

PEOPLE PLEASING

Another way women become bound with fear is being afraid of what others think of them. The Bible calls this **"the fear of man." (Proverbs 29:25 NIV)** and promises that it will become a snare to those who are preoccupied with it. When we worry about winning the approval of others, we are unable to move for fear of making someone unhappy or losing their friendship. Human relationships can restrict us from following Christ if we let people's view of us define who we are. Then we believe more in what people say than what God says.

This fear kept many Jews in Jesus' day from fully trusting in Christ. **"Even after Jesus had done all these miraculous signs in their presence, they still would not believe in him…because of the Pharisees they would not confess their faith for fear they would be put out of the synagogue; for they loved praise from men more than praise from God." (John 12:37-43 NIV)** These Jews gave in to the fear of rejection by prominent men. Even after seeing the miracles, the fear of man had a more powerful hold on them than the fear of God. Because of pride, we can be utterly terrified of what others may think of us. We want people to think well of us, so we live to keep their opinions high.

Much of the fear in people-pleasing comes from our own active imaginations about what people will do to us. Our fears are compounded by our own irrational beliefs about what everyone thinks. We selfishly assume that everyone is focused on us and, therefore, has an opinion. Realistically, everyone is more concerned with themselves to care about what we are doing!

I am not suggesting that we purposely ignore how we are coming across to people. What I am saying is that when we decide to live according the Spirit's leading, we will undoubtedly clash with many who are not following Christ. The Spirit and the flesh are always at odds. The early Apostles ruffled feathers wherever they went, living and preaching the truth with power. The Apostle Paul addressed the issue this way: **"Am I now trying to win the approval of man, or of God? Or am I trying to please men? If I were still trying to please men, I would not be a servant of Christ." (Galatians 1:10 NIV)** If we seek the approval of people in hopes of them liking us, then most likely their demands will pull us out of God's will. Conversely, if we live in good conscience towards God, we will probably suffer rejection and scorn from those who live by their own rules.

Overcoming the fear of man is a huge milestone in the Christian walk. We need to personally settle the matter of whom we are living to please. A.W. Tozer wrote about the courage needed to take a fierce stand to live for Christ. He assures us from his own experience that, if we supply the grit, then God will supply the grace![21]

SELF-PITY

Another fear that can defeat us in our Christian activity is self-pity. Self-pity comes from losing sight of God in the midst of suffering. It is feeling sorry for ourselves and then choosing to settle into that sorrow. We don't recognize what God has done or is doing because we are busy focusing on what He has not done!

The devil is right in our ear trying to steal our joy and hope. He knows that a person robbed of hope is like a deflated balloon. It just lays flat with no buoyancy for flight. He appeals to self by saying, "You are the only one suffering. Everyone else is having a nice life! What you are going through is horrible, and no one even cares!" We vocalize what the devil has told us by complaining and finding fault. Soon, we wind up with a testimony of how bad life is with God!

Self-pity can become competitive as we fall into a one-upmanship role in telling others about our problems. If someone is hurting, we hurt more. If someone's finances are failing, we are failing more. We are convinced that we are worse off than anyone else, so we compete for sympathy from others. I have watched women sabotage answers to their problems because they enjoyed the sound of their own complaining and the attention they get, rather than have a solution to their problem.

Self-pity can take us down to the point to where we fear getting well. Lying down in fear is easier than standing in faith. **"When Jesus saw him laying there and learned he had been in this condition for a long time, he asked him, 'Do you want to get well?'" (John 5:6 NIV)** Jesus was checking to see if the man's will had been crippled by self-pity. He knew that the man would have to adjust to doing for himself if he were healed. Jesus was asking him, "If God

---

21   Rut, Rot or Revival, p. 10

heals you, will you make the emotional adjustment to move on?" In the same way, we need to have the willingness to spring to our feet, ignoring our fears, when Jesus comes to deliver us from our difficulties.

LIVING IN THE LIGHT

As Christians, we need to grasp our potential of living free of fear. The fear of death is the basis for all other fears. It is the basement level upon which the Kingdom of Darkness is built. "Darkness" refers to that which is unknown, that which we don't understand, or uncertainty about the future. The power behind fear lies in the threat of death, harm, or punishment, and the mystery of the unknown. This veil of confusion creates such an anxiety in people that they become ruled by fear.

The Kingdom of Light is ruled by love. God demonstrated His love for us at Calvary where Jesus took the punishment of our sins and then conquered death by His resurrection. **"Since the children have flesh and blood, he too shared in their humanity so that by his death, he might destroy him who holds the power of death—that is the devil—and free those who all their lives were held in slavery by their fear of death." (Hebrews 2: 14-15 NIV)** The key to overcoming fear is trusting in Christ's power demonstrated by the resurrection. By that same power, God will lead us through our areas of uncertainty or darkness. We have to re-train our minds to believe what God has made known to us (light) rather than what we expect to happen based on lies (darkness).

The assurance of our eternal destiny is the basis for overcoming all fear. Faith in Jesus Christ takes away the pain of not knowing where we will go when we die. **"Where, O' death, is your sting?" (1 Corinthians 15:55 NIV)** If we can get over the fear of our own death, then every other fear is a lesser fear and, therefore, conquerable. Taking action based on faith by trusting in Christ's power overcomes avoidance behavior. Rational, scriptural thinking is this, "No matter what loss I am threatened with, it won't matter because ultimately I will be saved! Even if I die, I will be safe in Heaven forever!" Our faith in God can become stronger than our worst fears!

The Bible tells us that **"God does not give us a spirit of timidity, but a spirit of power, of love, and self-discipline."(1 Timothy 1:7 NIV)** God's power is activated when we step out in faith as He leads us. A godly confidence grows in us as we discover God's faithfulness again and again. We become so sure of Him that our assurance begins to show in our personality. **"Therefore, since we have such a hope, we are very bold!" (2 Corinthians 3:12 NIV)** Confidence is ours in Christ.

Finally, a close relationship with Jesus closes the gap of mystery that brings fear. **"But perfect love drives out fear..." (1 John 4:18 NIV)** We know Him well enough to dwell securely. As sin barriers are removed, we sense the vital, daily presence of God. Darkness from fear is driven out as we enjoy His guidance and love. This is yet another way we benefit from Christ's supremacy, knowing that He will handle every aspect of our daily life. We may not know how, but we definitely know Who.

∾ Chapter 11 ∾
IT GETS WORSE!

The design and coloring of the snake's skin are useful for camouflage; brown diamonds for desert rattlers and green striping for marsh-dwellers. Compatible with its environment, the snake blends in to resemble a tree branch, a green reed, or whatever is growing up around it. A passerby would have difficulty distinguishing the creature from its surroundings because of its natural disguise.

In the same way, sin causes Christians to blend in with the rest of the world. When we do the same things as unbelievers do, we remain hidden and do not stand out as God's special people. When our interests, conversations, and habits follow the earthly pattern, we lose our distinction as the new creatures in Christ that we really are. The following are some worldly ways that we wear as camouflage.

HARDNESS

The presence of sin hardens our inner being because self must stiffen to insist on having its own way. We can effectively resist God when we harden against Him. Thus we develop a harsh, staunch, self-defensive attitude. The more we ward off the Holy Spirit, the stronger the barriers form to protect our sin.

Hardness has a way of darkening our personality and there is little brightness or sparkle about us. Sin's effect on us is similar to having plaque on our teeth. A hard substance accumulates from daily chewing and incomplete cleaning that, if left untreated, invites decay and gum disease. In the same way, we need to recognize how evil has washed over our lives, sin habits that we have been chewing on, and attitudes we have adhered to which harden us.

As Christians, we cannot afford to be hardened and desensitized by sin. Sin and unbelief form a spiritual crowbar that Satan uses to pry us loose from our relationship with Christ. We should guard against offering him that wedge. **"See to it brothers, that none of you has a sinful, unbelieving heart that turns away from the living God. But encourage one another daily...so that none of you may be hardened by sin's deceitfulness." (Hebrews 3:12-13 NIV)** Let's consider several influences that can harden us.

Materialism

Materialism is an attitude that ignores spiritual values to focus on material gain. When we feed the desires of our selfish nature with possessions, we can become hardened by greed. We live for the here and now as if this world is all there is. Jesus taught about a man motivated by materialism. The rich merchant planned to have a nice life for himself for the remainder of his days. But God called him a fool and took his life warning, **"This is how it will be with anyone who stores up things for himself but is not rich toward God." (Luke 12:21 NIV)** This story describes the sin of hoarding, which is storing up for ourselves more than we could ever use. Hoarding is selfishness lavishly displayed.

One time I went with a friend to an open house of newly built mansions on one street. We were amazed at how every possible need was met with hot-tubs, televisions, stereos, appliances, expensive furniture, and plush carpeting. These homes were so cozy that the eventual owners would never want to leave them. They could be comfortably insulated from the world around them. Materialism has a way of insulating us, like the proverbial turtle in its shell. We can become so involved in our own nest-building that we have little time nor interest in activities that would make us rich towards God.

Suffering

Suffering is another occurrence in life that can harden us. We may feel the need to develop the hide of a rhino to survive these days. As Christians, our promised peace is constantly challenged by conflict. Why?

Life's hard circumstances are a result of God's curse upon the ground after Adam and Eve disobeyed. This judgment was meant to frustrate man's newly found independence, subjecting him to painful toil. This was also a redemptive measure to bring people to the end of themselves. With the right response to difficulty, people seek the Lord for relief.

But what if our response is different? What if we don't see God's redemptive purpose in our pain or, truthfully, don't want to? Perhaps we begrudge what has been allowed to happen to us, convinced that we have been singled out to suffer.

The Apostle Paul helps us to understand the underlying reason for suffering when he wrote: **"We were under great pressure, far beyond our ability to endure, so that we despaired even of life. Indeed, in our hearts we felt the sentence of death. But this happened that we might not rely on ourselves but on God, who raises the dead." (2 Corinthians 1:8-9 NIV)** Paul's difficulties forced him to rely on God alone and his outlook prevented him from resenting the ministry for which he suffered.

For whatever reason we suffer, angry resentful feelings will turn us to stone. Instead of becoming more pliable in brokenness, we will become immovable. Warren Wiersbe writes, "Nobody will deny that what happens to people is important. But what happens IN us will determine what happens THROUGH us."[22] When we harden to our circumstances, nothing happens through us. But when we let suffering take us to a new level of dependency on Christ, we soften as we surrender, allowing God's Spirit to work through us.

---

22 Why Us? When Bad Things Happen To God's People, p. 115

Lawlessness

As we brace ourselves to live in an increasingly dangerous world, the third influence that can harden us is lawlessness. New waves of violence raise the caution level of people, causing us to turn away from our fellow man for fear of personal harm. **"Because of the increase of wickedness, the love of most will grow cold..." (Matthew 24:12 NIV)**

A story in the paper told of a 15 year old boy who was shot and killed when he attempted to break up a fight involving his friend. Surprisingly, the fight was not gang-related, but between two mothers feuding over what their children had said to each other.[23] Headlines like these would make any would-be hero think twice about getting involved.

Incidents like this take place because people see lawlessness as a main theme at the movies or television. Hardness develops within us when we amuse ourselves by watching violence. The viewer must first train himself not to empathize, which is the intellectual identification of oneself with another, or else the violent scenes would bother him too much. The viewer's reasoning tells his mind, "It's not real." This habit of viewing puts people out of touch with reality. Genuine compassion is lost when people enjoy seeing others get hurt.

Lawlessness also visits us in the form of sensuality. Exposure to sensuality hardens our emotions into lust. **"...Because of the ignorance that is in them due to the hardening of their hearts. Having lost all sensitivity, they have given themselves over to sensuality..." (Ephesians 4:18-19 NIV)** We fool ourselves when we think we can handle explicit sexual scenes. Those images stick in our minds and eventually change us in our heart. When sensuality grips a life, sensitivity is lost.

Sensitivity

The Holy Spirit is at work, though, to remove stoniness from our hearts. **"I will give them an undivided heart and put a new spirit**

23   *The Plain Dealer*, Sept. 1996

in them; I will remove from them their heart of stone and give them a heart of flesh." (Ezekiel 11: 19-20 NIV) God clearly wants to be close to his people. Intimacy with God creates a heightened sensitivity for spiritual things. Our hearts are filled with an unexplainable warmth as He enables us to love. With hardness removed, we should have a special awareness of God and enjoy experiencing Him constantly.

PASSIVITY

Sin makes us passive. We just don't want to put forth the effort to seek God and follow His ways. As laziness and complacency bog us down in our will, our Christian life is diluted and dulled. Passivity includes dispositions such as apathy, disinterest, and lack of enthusiasm. Sin issues rob us of the motivation to reach for our high calling in Christ. We want God to make things easy for us and scorn the strengthening that comes from a struggle. Consequently, we put off Christian disciplines because they seem like too much work. To attempt anything better, greater, or higher is too much trouble, so we passively settle for the ordinary.

The natural inclination of the flesh is to shun self-discipline and enjoy self-indulgence. **"People will be lovers of themselves... without self-control...lovers of pleasure rather than lovers of God." (2 Timothy 3:3-4 NIV)** We prefer to be pampered. We give up so easily in our Christian service saying, "I just don't feel like it!" rather than press through feelings to complete our obligation.

The first place we need to look for passivity is in our daily devotion time. Are we reading the Bible daily? Are we seeking God through His Word? Is that appointment time with Jesus Christ important to us? This is the main way that God speaks to our heart. Do we want His direction or do we consider Bible reading a bother and a bore?

Next, do we really expect God to work? Are we waiting in faith or have we adopted a "God's not doin' nothin'!" attitude? Perhaps our lack of expectation merely a reflection of our own spiritual dullness. **"I will search Jerusalem with lamps and punish those who** are complacent…who think, 'The Lord will do nothing, either good or bad.'" (Zephaniah 1:12 NIV)** Those who are stagnant in heart don't expect anything from God; their faith is blotted out by their own sense of futility.

Thirdly, we look for inward passivity when we experience outward physical fatigue. Sin makes us tired! **"Our offenses and sins weigh us down and we are wasting away because of them. How then can we live?" (Ezekiel 33:10 NIV)** I vividly remember how sin had sapped my strength when I was running. Although I was in my mid-twenties and in perfect health, I had no power to run because of the load I was carrying within me. We need to find out if our chronic fatigue is due to a lack of vitamins, sleep and exercise or if our listlessness comes from a heavy heart weighed down with sin.

Passivity reminds me of the time I watched a middle-aged businessman run full speed down the sidewalk of a city street. I assumed he had an urgent appointment as he looked at his watch. Then he looked around to see who was watching and slowed down. He also remembered that he had an image to keep. So which should he keep, the image or the appointment? He couldn't keep both.

This is the same inner struggle we have in our commitment to God. Breaking into a full run to seek God and keeping that pace is often painful, awkward, and seemingly foolish. Self opts to be leisurely, play it safe, and not work up a sweat.

A work of repentance, though, can release Christians to seek God with zeal. The flame of zeal glows like a flare in the night when we abandon ourselves to the cause of Christ. Jesus said, **"I have come to bring fire on the earth, and how I wish it were already kindled!" (Luke 12:49 NIV)** Jesus came to ignite hearts with love for God. He longs to see passionate zeal burning within His people. We need to shake loose from the passivity of sin and break loose into a full run for our appointment with Christ.

SIN IS LEGAL GROUND

Satan's domain or realm of activity is darkness which consists of lies, unforgiveness, secret ways, and disobedience. Unconfessed, unrenounced sin is also within his domain and establishes "legal ground" by which he can oppress us. To agree with sin is to disagree with God. Any agreement we have with sin gives Satan spiritual permission to bring power against us. As an example, because of all my unconfessed sin during my depression, I was literally being held down from within by the enemy.

Another name of Satan is "Beelzebub" which means "Prince of Demons" or "Lord of the Flies." His name gives a graphic picture of his activity. Flies locate food in open garbage by an acute sense of smell. There, they land and lay eggs which hatch into maggots. In the same way, sin is spiritual garbage within us. Evil forces are offered a breeding ground when our life has not been cleansed by repentance. **"When an evil spirit come out of a man it goes through arid places...then it says "I will return to the house I left...Then it takes seven other spirit spirits more wicked than itself, and they go and live there."" (Matthew 12:43-45 NIV)**

Because our inner cleanliness reflects how much we agree with God, we are told to **"make every effort to be found spotless." (2 Peter 3:14 NIV)** It is clearly God's will that we rid ourselves of inner garbage so that we might be **"a radiant church, without stain or wrinkle or any other blemish, but holy and blameless." (Ephesians 5:27 NIV)** To be able to do that, let's look at the two types of sins mentioned here: "stains" and "wrinkles."

Stains

The stains in our life would be our own moral filth which are those selfish, wrong actions and attitudes which we have chosen to participate in by giving in to temptation. Most likely, those acts are numerous and diverse. If we stop to think, some sins will easily come to mind while others will require a reminder from God. The Apostle Paul gave a list of stains he considered to be obvious: **"sexual immorality, impurity and debauchery, idolatry and witchcraft; hatred, discord, jealousy, fits of rage, selfish ambition, dissensions, factions, and envy..." (Galatians 5:19-20 NIV)**

One of the most common types of stains is unforgiveness. God's nature is to use His power to release people from their offenses through forgiveness. The basis for God's grace is His love. God chose to love us above the offenses we committed against Him. As His children, God has power available for us to do the same. An attitude that holds an angry grudge against another person does not reflect His nature. When we participate in unforgiveness, we are essentially saying that, even though God stands willing to forgive, we do not. This hard attitude sets up legal ground for the enemy to work in our lives. Developing a mindset to willingly forgive as situations arise will keep us free from the devil's invasion and help us to discover new depths of love available through Christ.

Wrinkles

The wrinkles in our life can be described as damage we have suffered from the hand of others. Many times people have forced their ways upon us, behaving as intruders. Afterwards, these intruders leave sin wounds or places where they have hurt us emotionally. The devil will watch for these areas of weakness as entry points to invade us. **"Tyre has said to Jerusalem, 'Aha! The gate to the nations is broken and its doors have swung open to me, not that she lies in ruin I will prosper.'" (Ezekiel 26:2 NIV)** Rejection and criticism from others can cause lasting damage to our inner being. Enemy forces will try to compound that damage.

In her excellent book, *Beauty For Ashes*, Joyce Meyer describes the abuse that many suffer from living in a corrupted world. She explains, "I believe that most people are abused in one way or another during their lifetime… God created people for love and acceptance, but the devil works hard to keep us feeling rejected."[24]

The Holy Spirit can reveal to us the depth of our hurt, and then cleanse and heal our sin wounds. **"The Lord builds up Jerusalem; he gathers the exiles. He heals the brokenhearted and binds up their wounds." (Psalm 147:2-3 NIV)** Getting rid of feelings of rejection and woundedness depends on seeing the truth about

---

24   Beauty For Ashes, p. 9

what our intruders did to us. With stains, darkness remains intact by denying what we have done. But with wrinkles, darkness remains through shame, guilt, and denial of the damage we have suffered. If we can face up to the awfulness of our experiences, then Jesus will bring healing to close up those sin wounds.

One type of wrinkle that we need to be aware of is generational sin, a habitual sin that settles in a family and is passed on as a trait. For example, I had been seeking God to disclose legal ground in my life when he showed me generational sin in my own family.

One of my cousins had written a biography of my great-grandfather as a matter of historical interest to the family. He was a devout atheist and avid reader of the writings of Charles Darwin. As the father of twelve children, he chose to intrude on his family as a wife-beater and child abuser. Most of the daughters developed character traits of hatred and rebellion from the harsh treatment they received growing up. My grandmother suffered from clinical depression most of her adult life.

I could see those same dispositions taking hold in my own personality. Through prayer, I identified and confessed these generational traits, and asked God's forgiveness to halt any further outworking of this sin. I chose not have to conform to family traits that were passed on, finding the cross of Jesus Christ as the perfect barrier for generational sin.

SPIRITUAL WARFARE

We can emerge from blending into the backdrop of the world with willingness of God's' people to fight evil through spiritual warfare. Repentance is ground-level spiritual warfare. When we seek God's deliverance from the evil we see in ourselves, we are taking action against Satan by prying his grip off our lives.

I admire the cave lady from the comic strip "B.C." who raises her club in a flurry of whammings at the slightest hint of the serpent's presence. Our reaction to evil should be the same. God wants us to develop a hatred for sin and evil because they are against His holy nature. **"Let those who love the Lord hate evil." (Psalm 97:10 NIV)**

The devil has worked to build his structure of darkness in the hearts of each of us. When we come to Christ, these structures or strongholds need to be brought down and replaced by God's stronghold which is Christlikeness.

To illustrate the inner work that needs to be done, we can compare the demolition of the Sands Hotel in Las Vegas. Americans celebrated the 1997 New Year by watching the televised implosion of this world-famous gambling casino. At the stroke of midnight, a well-engineered inner explosion reduced the hotel to rubble within minutes. The owners had plans to build a 6,000 room mega-resort on the same 63 acre site. The old structure had to be destroyed in order to build the new one on the same site. [25]

Jesus spoke of an inner violence experienced by those who work to rid themselves of Satan's strongholds. **"From the days of John the Baptist until now, the kingdom of heaven had been forcefully advancing and forceful men lay hold of it." (Matthew 11:12 NIV)** The kingdom of heaven is within us. It forcefully advances when we invite God to implode or demolish enemy strongholds. These are habitual thinking patterns that are contrary to the truth. The power of His truth brings the old structure of lies crashing down. Then God will build truth in us on the same site. **"Therefore, if anyone is in Christ, he is a new creation; the old is gone, the new has come!" (2 Corinthians 5:17 NIV)** When legal ground is removed, the enemy no longer has power to oppress us. God then builds His ways into us, transforming us inwardly to Christlikeness.

---

25   *The Wall Street Journal*, May, 1996

∾ Chapter 12 ∾
REBELLION

The white-turbaned snake charmer sits cross-legged before a rising coiled cobra that is mysteriously enchanted by the music flowing from the man's flute. In the same unexplainable way, America was charmed by the sounds of screaming electric guitars and bass drums during the mid 1960's. The lyrics from those songs became the provocative voice that urged youth to rise up against the established political, social, and moral systems in society. The essence of this movement is described in the Bible as **"the spirit who is now at work in those who are disobedient." (Ephesians 2:2 NIV)** For some reason, this spirit was welcomed and well organized in the 60's. Now after 30 years, we have yet to wash its taste from our mouths.

New Age specialist Gary North makes this observation: "Many of the changes wrought philosophically and morally from the counter-culture are still with us…the hippies got haircuts, but a significant proportion of them have not changed their world view."[26] I have met people who admit to being stuck in the 60's. They hold that time period so dear that it becomes a reference point in their lives. Their loyalty to the banner cry of "sex, drugs, and rock-n-roll" speaks of a gut-level sympathy for personal rebellion. Disobedience has become an accepted norm in our culture thanks to the 60's. Rebellion was loosed across this land in the name of peace and love, and we are finding the results to be anything but charming.

---

26   Unholy Spirits, p. 4

As Christians, we need to question if the ideals of the 60's perhaps shaped our own view of authority, validating our own personal rebellion. Exactly how much do we agree with those ideals? Are we convinced that rebellion is wrong, or do we hold to our right to defy given authority? Do we honestly believe that defiance is sin, or are we intrigued by its spunk?

We need to look closely at this mind-set mainly because the consequences are so detrimental. Rebellious thinking can virtually ruin our lives and relationship with God. After seeing the truth about rebellion, perhaps we would be willing to take that long and winding road back to our senses.

KORAH'S REBELLION

The anarchy of the 60's can be seen on a smaller scale in the revolt led by Korah against Moses. Moses had given the law to Israel along with the system of sacrificial worship that the Lord had commanded. These moral restrictions were something which Israel, now like a bridled horse, had to get used to.

Before long, those who resented the commandments and religious restraints voiced their opinion. **"Korah, son of Izhar and certain Reubenites—Dathan and Abiram...became insolent and rose up against Moses." (Numbers 16:1-2 NIV)** They were angry about being told what to do with no say-so. We will see why these actions were wrong along with the resulting consequences.

False Reasoning

Rebellion rises up from the false reasoning of self-domination. We assume that we are entitled to govern our own lives and have the right to live however we want. This reasoning does not reflect or agree with the Creator's perspective.

We must see ourselves as creatures who have been formed by God and given breath. Therefore, we are subject to the wishes of the Creator. We do not have the right nor the proper ability to govern ourselves. As part of God's creation, we are under His supervision. Any societal institutions such as government, family, commerce, or corporate religious worship have been designed by God to keep order, and should be willingly observed.

An attitude of rebellion questions the right of authorities to enforce order. "What right do they have to tell me what to do?" This habit of questioning rather than accepting given authority becomes deeply imbedded in our hearts until it affects all of our actions. We insist on doing everything our own way. People who breeze through red lights go against the authority of traffic laws. The rebel becomes incensed about anyone infringing on his personal rights as an individual. He does not consider the overall benefit of having order in society.

Doubt and unbelief also cause us to distrust authority. In the 60's, there was a slogan, "Don't trust anyone over thirty!" Our inner decision to distrust those in authority causes us to ignore their directives. Selfish pride whispers, "They don't know what they are talking about! I know more than they do."

Rebellion also breeds an attitude of defiance. **"Then Moses summoned Dathan and Abiram...But they said, 'We will not come!'" (Numbers 16:12 NIV)** When we set our will to defend our rights, then we will refuse to do what we are told. The underlying personal vow of rebellion is, "Nobody tells ME what to do!" In the 60's, the hippies refused to get haircuts, to shave, to bathe, and to get jobs. They thought they were proving their point through pro- test, but actually they were making life harder for themselves. Delib- erate refusal to do what we are told makes us very hard to get along with. Because rebellion is a dysfunction of the will, it will misguide us with unreasonable decisions wherever we go.

When a person hardens his will with "I won't," he resents doing even simple tasks. Resentment binds up our activities, causing us to begrudge everything we do. Outwardly we may be going through the motions of doing our work, but inwardly we are resisting with all our might. We struggle in our emotions unnecessarily because we are so put out. As long as we resent a voice other than our own directing us, we will have difficulty in quietly following along doing what we are told.

God's View

God will not endorse a rebellious attitude. Don't look for Him to take our side when we stand in defiance of our authorities. He has set a system of authority on earth, choosing to accomplish His purposes in an orderly fashion. **"Everyone must submit himself to the governing authorities, for there is no authority except that which God has established. The authorities that exist have been established by God. Consequently, he who rebels against the authority is rebelling against what God has instituted, and those who do so bring judgment on themselves." (Romans 13:1-2 NIV)** When we rebel against the structures of government that God has set in place, we are in effect rebelling against God Himself. By our own choice, we are setting ourselves up for judgment and will receive the due consequences as God sees fit.

Furthermore, God will not supply grace to enable rebellion. If we decide to act in this manner, we will have to use a different power source other than God. Rebellion is **"like the sin of divination" (1 Samuel 15:23 NIV)** or like witchcraft because people resort to using sinful power to get their way. With strong, worked-up emotions, they use emotional self-will power to energize their rebellion.

The rebellious must also seek out sympathizers, as did Korah, to help find strength in numbers. People spread their moral outrage to others by leading others in rebellion. All these actions combined can lead to a very heavy emotional overload. We live on shaky spiritual ground when we live in rebellion and we are in for a fall when God decides it is time to deal with our sin.

PARENTS AND CHILDREN

The Bible gives specific teaching on obedience in several main relationships. The first relationship is between parents and children. **"Children, obey your parents in the Lord, for this is right. Honor your father and mother—which is the first command with a promise—that it may go well with you and that you may enjoy long life on the earth." (Ephesians 6:1-3 NIV)** The way we decide to relate to our parents will set the pattern for every other relation-

102

ship we have. In this verse we are told to do what they tell us and treat them with respect. If we have the proper humble attitude towards our parents, our stay on earth will be smoother and less frustrating. I can't emphasize this teaching enough because it is so life changing. The fact that Jesus obeyed his imperfect earthly parents show us that this is how we receive training to relate to given authority.

However, if we are resentful of our parent's rule, then the opposite of this verse is also true and things will not go well with us. Rebellious children who work up the nerve to defy their parents will, later on, give no thought to talking back to the teacher, the boss, the preacher, the policeman, the judge, etc. The behavior we learn at home we will carry through life.

The most common catalyst of rebellion among children is harsh or cruel authority because it frustrates the child's heart. **"Fathers, do not exasperate your children." (Ephesians 6:4 NIV)** When a child, who naturally wants to please his parents, is met with angry, unjust discipline then he will give up trying. That parent has seriously betrayed that child's trust. The child will look to his own resources and use rebellion as a way of fighting back.

Growing up under harsh authority causes much damage to the child's inner being, distorting his need for love and acceptance. I once knew a man whose father beat the children regularly after nights of drinking. One of the sons rebelled so badly that he removed himself from society, living on welfare in Alaska.

If our parents made poor choices while raising us, the most important truth we can believe is Christ's ability to make all things new. As Christians, God has healing power for those who find the courage to trust His promises. Rather than lay blame, we can be raised up from our disappointments. God has power to transform even the most heart-wrenching of family cases. We must give Christ a chance to use His creative ability to straighten out what was twisted and bent within us. He will prove how He can work through less-than-perfect parents to accomplish His will for us.

SLAVES AND MASTERS

The next area that avails itself to rebellion is the workplace. **"Slaves, obey your earthly masters with respect and fear, and with sincerity of heart, just as you would obey Christ." (Ephesians 6:5 NIV)** This seems like a tall order with the added pressure on employees from company downsizing and layoffs. Yet this was originally written to include actual slaves who probably never tasted fairness, and yet were still asked to obey. Obedience to supervisors in the workplace is an earthly tool God uses to teach us His supremacy. Although we are doing what the company tells us, we are obeying for the sake of Christ.

The workplace is often an unrewarding, ungracious place where pressure builds for people. This atmosphere creates an incubator for the defense of personal rights and, hence, rebellion. Generally, employers don't have time to understand employees' problems. Conversely, employees don't see the big picture; they only see their small part that magnifies their personal needs. Despite the misunderstandings, we must do our jobs. This economy is a given system in which we must operate. Our saving grace to get through each work day will only come as we adhere to Biblical principles.

Having worked for difficult bosses, I have learned the secret of obedience that has helped me transcend their particular personalities. First, I had to give up my ideas about what was fair. Equity in the workload usually gives way to who is willing to do the work. Many bosses will take the path of least resistance just to get the job done. Even though this may mean doing more work, we can't get caught up in insisting on fairness to the point where we rebel against what we are told to do. God is considering our heart at all times.

Next, I had to get over resenting how things were said to me. I mentally sort through the demanding or demeaning tone of voice to hear what is being asked of me. I try to focus on the directive rather than become entangled in the emotions of how I felt when someone was purposely mean. It takes a degree of discipline to say to yourself, "It doesn't matter how you feel—just do it!"

Finally, I learned that my schedule is not my own. I am being paid by someone to do a job for them, so it is useless to become angry about what I am asked to do. I have to yield, even when asked to do additional work. When I let God determine my schedule, I become expectant of small but significant breakthroughs to get my job done.

WOMEN AND MEN

The last area we will look at is rebellion between women and men, wives and husbands. **"Wives, submit to your husband as to the Lord. For the husband is the head of the wife as Christ is head of the Church." (Ephesians 5:22-23 NIV) "But the woman is the glory of man." (1 Corinthians 11:7 NIV)**

One of the major areas where the mood of the 60's stirred up discontent was in the role of women in society. Without undercutting important reforms won in the 1930's such as the right to vote, own property, and enter the college of their choice, the "Women's Movement" of the 1970's unleashed a destructive force aimed not only to elevate women but also to trample men.

Groping to label the problem of felt unfulfillment among American housewives, leading feminists agreed to name the unseen enemy "patriarchy" or "rule of the father." From her research, Mary A. Kassian writes, "Feminists reasoned that the demise of patriarchy would bring about women's fulfillment. Liberating women from patriarchy would allow women to become whole."[27] The feminists who acted upon this reasoning lead a mass rebellion against men.

When women rebel against men they often compete for the position of authority. Displacement and replacement are always the goals of rebellion. Filled with distrust, they maneuver to take matters into their own hands. For example, Mary Ann went on vacation to the Bahamas with several of her girlfriends. They decided to rent a sailboat and hire a captain to take them around the islands. Mary Ann sails somewhat and likes to scuba dive. She is also a staunch feminist. She accused the captain of treating her like she was stupid

27   The Feminist Gospel, p. 24

because he gave her some directions. Actually, she resented being told what to do. But the rule of the sea is that a boat has only one captain. She tells how she defied him: "I just took my bathing suit top off and flung it down because I was mad!" So was bra-burning a popular form of protest back in the 70's. I guess we really showed them who was boss, didn't we?

In the home, the wife is required to submit to the husband. The husband is like the captain of the ship, responsible to direct and guide the family. The problem comes when the wife distrusts authority and decides to wrench control out of her husband's hands. I talked to a young wife who was really struggling with the principle of submission. I asked her to just try to go along with what her husband decided. She told me the thought of it made her sick to her stomach! Probably so. It is true that a part of us dies when we give in to the wishes of another. Self prefers to dominate rather than submit. But this is an area where we can step out in faith to trust and believe God's Word. He will bring godly order in the home when we comply with His wishes.

DUE CONSEQUENCES

Korah was given a chance to reconsider his actions, but refused to fear God and repent. **"So they moved away from the tents of Korah, Dathan, and Abiram...As soon as he finished saying all this, the ground under them split apart, the earth opened its mouth and swallowed them...they went down alive into the grave...the earth closed over them and they perished and were gone from the community." (Numbers 16:27:33 NIV)** Korah, his family and friends received fatal consequences for his rebellious opposition to Moses.

I believe this judgment is similar to the way a person feels when suffering from depression. Having experienced its symptoms, I know that depression is like being buried alive. Life's concerns seem to cave in on a person, making the slightest task extremely difficult. Like a living death, the future seems to be bleak with no reason to go on.

Minereth and Meier Clinic reports that "a majority of Americans suffer from serious clinical depression…according to one estimate about twenty million persons in America between the ages of eighteen and seventy are currently depressed."[28] Research says that a majority of Americans are depressed. Is this the price America must pay for her rebellious heyday? During the 60's, was the "spirit of disobedience" looking ahead with premeditated malice by tempting Americans to dump their authorities, knowing full well that the spiritual ground would open up and swallow them?

To attribute the whole cause of depression to inner rebellion would be too simple an explanation for such a complicated condition. But I believe that a root of rebellion produces other wrong attitudes that compound our problems to bring us down. With this example from Bible history, we can recognize God's displeasure with disobedience and His readiness to act in order to back up those He has positioned in authority.

BENDING THE WILL

The main reason why we need to be healed in our will is because rebellion injures our relationship and service to God. We become disqualified from greater spiritual challenges because we won't obey. **"For there are rebellious people…they claim to know God, but by their actions they deny him. They are detestable, disobedient and unfit for doing anything good." (Titus 1:10-16 NIV)**

When God speaks to His people, He uses direct commands such as, "Do this!" If we bristle when we receive a direct command then we will struggle with doing what we have been told. Our will needs to be bent to hear and obey. We must recognize the value of listening and acting upon what we are told.

We need to be assured that God's authority is a loving, controlled rule. He never vents out of uncontrolled anger. We can trust His motives in looking out for us. **"I am the good shepherd. The good shepherd lays down his life for his sheep." (John 10:11 NIV)**

---

28 Happiness Is A Choice, p. 20

Lastly, we rob ourselves of God's blessing when we persist in this attitude. Life is so much harder when we refuse to obey. **"But the rebellious live in a parched land." (Psalm 68:6 NRSV)** Our prayers and petitions to God can be sweetly and consistently answered when we outgrow these defiant ways. Jesus Himself was heard by the Father because of His reverent submission. We can open our lives to receive God's blessing when we learn to stop fighting and start following, putting down our own personal rebellion.

∽ Chapter 13 ∽
THAT WOMAN JEZEBEL

Our eyes are opened to a bigger picture of evil forces organized against us when we read: **"For our struggle is not against flesh and blood, but against the authorities, against the powers of this dark world and against the spiritual forces of evil in the heavenly realms." (Ephesians 6:12 NIV)** These forces work to exert influence so that evil will be played out in people's lives. The devil wants people to become extreme in their sin. To illustrate, in Malaysia a 23 foot python was found strangling a man and attempting to swallow him whole. This gruesome headline shows us sin's goal to overpower and consume us. The sobering truth is that the devil has a plan for supremacy in all things, too.

THE STRATEGY AGAINST US

I believe the devil has drawn a collective "bull's eye" target on the lives of women to implement his plan. Since the beginning he has set his sights on Eve, targeting her mind with his suggestions. The devil knows that if he can fill a woman's "container" with enough sin, it will distort her complex emotional system, and she will be virtually impossible to live with. **"It is better to live in a desert land than with a quarrelsome, ill-tempered woman." (Proverbs 21:19 NIV)** The underlying strategy is to create such animosity, competition, and strife in the home that it will become a place of pain for family members. Breaking up families is what the devil wants, and he is doing it subtly from the inside.

Scripture gives us the necessary insight to see this strategy being worked against us. To understand it, we must take a hard look at "the woman Jezebel," Satan's woman of sin. Queen Jezebel was the murderous, controlling wife of King Ahab who legalized idolatry in Israel and killed many of the Lord's prophets. She was a terror! There is no other woman described in the Bible who gave herself so completely to do evil. **"There was never a man like Ahab, who sold himself to do evil in the eyes of the Lord, urged on by Jezebel his wife." (1 Kings 21:25 NIV)**

She is mentioned again in the book of Revelation as John recounts his vision of Christ. In the vision, Jesus gave a message to the church of Thyatira, **"Nevertheless, I have this against you: you tolerate that woman Jezebel, who calls herself a prophetess." (Revelation 2:20 NIV)** The person of Jezebel was long dead, so we know that Jesus was referring to the personality of Jezebel being duplicated in the lives of church members. They were tolerating the woman Jezebel by allowing her evil traits in their behavior.

The problem of Jezebel did not stop with the early church; the problem with "her" is ongoing. Satan's forces are still busy tempting women to sin to such a degree that they mimic Jezebel's character. Time Magazine observes today's prevailing attitude among women: "But if feminism of the 60's and 70's was steeped in research and obsessed with social change, feminism today is wed to the culture of celebrity and self-obsession…It's also true that women are joining together…and that we now have 'girl power', that sassy, don't-mess-with-me adolescent spirit that Madison Avenue carefully caters to."[29] As women adapt to what they see around them, the standards for female behavior drop lower and lower, while the divorce rate climbs higher and higher.

Satan's plan is working like a charm in the world, but is it also having some degree of success in the Church? I believe that it is. I also strongly believe it is time for Christian women to honestly check their own toleration of the Jezebel spirit to see what influence it is having in their lives. Perhaps by describing this personality

29 *Time Magazine*, June 29m 1998

pattern in fuller detail, we may discern its ways and repent. For our own good, we can spare ourselves and loved ones of the emotional pain that the Jezebel spirit brings.

PERSONAL POWER

One of the earmarks of Jezebel is her lust for personal power. Women who suffer from deep felt insecurities may decide to prove themselves through emotional power-plays.   Mainly, they want to feel important by having people answer to them. This is seen in the home when women use forceful behavior to dominate. Jezebel saw her chance to rule Israel through Ahab. When he failed to obtain a plot of land he wanted, she had the property owner murdered and then seized the land. In essence, she told her husband, "Get out of the way! I'll handle it!" This effectively sent a message to Israel's leadership—obey her or else! **"So the elders and nobles who lived in Naboth's city did as Jezebel directed in the letter she had written them." (1 Kings 21:11 NIV)**

We see this same tactic used in the home as the wife watches for her husband's weakness, and then uses it against him. She wants to be the boss, so she undermines his authority to have her own way. She enjoys the sense of personal power she gains from leading the family. The husband who gives in to her becomes a figurehead, like Ahab, who merely carries out her orders.

STRIFE

Because Jezebel establishes her rule by force, living with her means having an atmosphere of strife as she contends for her ground. **"'How can there be peace,' Jehu replied, 'As long as the idolatry and witchcraft of your mother abound?'" (2 Kings 9:22 NIV)** The character of Jezebel is unreasonable and divisive. She enjoys arguing and is at her best during a fight! Her weapons are harsh, cutting words and accusations that are meant to hurt. She knows that arguing shuts down communication, but she doesn't care because to win is to rule. As tension hangs in the air, people know that they have a potential gorilla on their hands if they cross her.

MANIPULATION

Under the influence of Jezebel, a woman becomes a master at manipulation, scheming, and control. **"The hearts of the people are filled with schemes to do wrong." (Ecclesiastes 8:11 NIV)** Manipulation is the use of emotional ploys to get others to do what we want. We make plans in our minds, "If I say this then so-and-so will do that" or "If I start to cry then he will give in to me."

We manipulate when we bear down on others to impose our expectations of them. Selfish control of others is a form of inter-personal slavery. We enslave others by forcing our will upon them, requiring them to serve us. The Bible describes manipulation this way: **"I find more bitter than death the woman who is a snare, whose heart is a trap and whose hands are chains." (Ecclesiastes 7:26 NIV)** Woman can misuse love by using their sexual abilities as a manipulative tool. They use their soft voice and nurturing skills to make false promises of love and get people to do what they want.

Insecurities can also cause women to resort to possessive behavior with family members and friends. Ownership seems to cure their need to build themselves up. We may offer a shoulder to keep people dependent on us, or act helplessly dependent to keep people involved in helping us. Either way, we guard those we attempt to control, counting people, positions, or ministry as "mine!"

CONTROL THROUGH DISAPPROVAL

One of Jezebel's most effective control methods is the use of rejection through disapproval. She draws people to herself, trying to get them to please her in exchange for her love and approval. When loved ones try to do things for her, they are turned down because she refuses to be pleased. She fusses over petty details, letting them know they are never good enough to be accepted by her.

"I don't like this and I don't like that!" she complains. She lures people into the bondage of people-pleasing, leaving them with a sense of rejection, discouragement, and hopelessness with her relentless use of disapproval.

I once read a biography about the incredibly talented, award-winning singer/actress Barbra Streisand. She told how she still has a tough time winning her mother's hard won approval.[30] Don't kill yourself, Barbra, it doesn't do any good. Some people are never pleased. Those who purposely withhold acceptance and approval from loved ones are following Jezebel in her insidious use of control.

One such woman was King David's wife, Michal, who used this tactic on the king after she watched him celebrate the return of the ark of God in their midst. The ark carried God's presence. David gladly entered into worship, but Michal remained at a distance, watching from an upper window. That's what sin does; it keeps us at a distance from God's presence.

She hated him for his happiness, yet refused to come down and enjoy the moment for herself. **"Michal, daughter of Saul watched from a window. And when she saw King David leaping and dancing before the Lord, she despised him in her heart." (2 Samuel 6:16 NIV)** This was a terribly unhappy woman expressing her unhappiness. Women under the influence of Jezebel hate true Christian joy because it so sharply contrasts with their life of misery from their sin.

Later, Michal's reticent attitude, like a spiritual wet blanket effectively quenched the King's exuberance and desire to bless his family. This is like the Christian wife who squashes her husband's excitement and vision with negative comments when he comes home from a ministry event. She purposely withholds her approval to keep his enthusiasm and motivation in check. Her agenda is to control him. This attitude cools relationships quickly. King David chose never to come near Michal again. Her own disapproval and contempt left her a lonely, barren woman until her death.

---

30   Streisand, The Pictorial Biography, p. 12

QUEEN MOTHER

Pride and disdain fills the life of the women who tolerates Jezebel because she sees herself as "Queen." **"In her heart she boasts, 'I sit as a queen...'" (Revelation 18:7 NIV)**

She acts out this fantasy with a cold, demeaning manner, talking down to people as if they were children. She wants to preside over situations and can be very bossy, yet fearful of having any direct responsibility. Making others serve her is more her style.

Her greatest fear is seeing the truth about herself. She has built up an image in her mind as the loving, caring "Queen Mother." She hates repentance because she does not want to consider her own sin. That would show the image to be a lie. She does not like to be told she has a problem because she sees everyone else as having the problem. **"This is the way of the adulteress: she eats and wipes her mouth and says, 'I've done nothing wrong.'" (Proverbs 30:20 NIV)**

Sin in the heart that is buried beneath self-satisfaction cannot be unearthed. Women under the influence of Jezebel hide behind a guise of self-righteousness. They will bring terrible damage to relationships, treating people shamefully, and yet pretend to be sweet and loving. Illusive, like Jekyll and Hyde, this is the mysterious behavior of Jezebel. **"You have trusted in your wickedness and have said, 'No one sees me!'" (Isaiah 47:10 NIV)**

But God sees it. He sees it all. He sees what we do, how we think, and who we are. And someday we will have to answer to Him for how we have lived. **"Nothing in all creation is hidden from God's sight. Everything is uncovered and laid bare before His eyes of him to whom we must give account." (Hebrews 4:13 NIV)** Isn't it time we stop to consider the future? Can't we see that the way we live is important? Do we see that following the ways of Jezebel gains us nothing that will last? We need to realize that, when the eyes of God focus on us at the final judgment, He will be searching for Christ in us. Will Christ be seen as the One supremely ruling from the center of our life or the mis-guided rule of a false "Queen?"

CHARLENE

I speak from experience on this topic because I have had many opportunities to observe the Jezebel spirit actively operating in people. More and more I find women conforming to this pattern of behavior as they harden in their sin. Probably the most significant experience that proves all I have said was when I met Charlene.

The last thing I expected on my new job was to be involved in a spiritual power struggle. My interview with the office manager had been friendly enough, but the welcome quickly faded when I was introduced to my co-worker whose desk was next to mine. I'll call her "Charlene."

A petite, dark-haired Italian woman in her mid-twenties, she was attractive, wore expensive clothes, and spoke in a low tone of voice. The first day, she went out of her way to get me a cup of coffee and explain office procedures. But by the end of the week, the friendliness had soured and I sensed something strange about the relationships in the office. The other women were hesitant to make friends with me, as if doing so might break some pact of loyalty with Charlene. Although she was not management, everyone seemed seek her approval.

It didn't take long to see how gossip and slander were rampant in the office. Long, whispering personal phone calls had priority over business calls for Charlene. Many of the calls were to organize the many drinking parties she planned for the weekends. Her hold on the other employees was with the sin they were involved with when they partied with her.

After a couple of weeks, through innuendoes and control tactics, she let me know that she ruled the office, although nothing was actually said. I clearly resisted her expectations to cater to her and that's when the "war" broke out between us.

Soon, she coerced another employee to complain about me and I was called into the manager's office. Fortunately, he laughed it off. But I found out later that Charlene was right on the heels of that incident trying to convince him to fire me because she said that I wasn't working out! With mean tactics like this, work became very stressful. I never knew what she would do next to try to discredit me. Besides that, her mood swings were very unnerving. Sometimes she would really apply herself at work. Then, something would upset her and she would fly into a rage, screaming, cursing, and blaming others, especially me. One day after an outburst, she told me that she didn't know what came over her during those temper fits; when the anger took hold of her she couldn't control herself.

My mind was racing to understand what was going on. I thought how similar Charlene's personality was to the raging woman office manager I had worked for at the photography studio. I was facing another "Queen Mother" figure in this office. I thought I had walked away from that problem years ago. But Charlene had everyone walking on eggshells just like the other woman had done. The pattern was identical. Was it possible that the same evil I had recognized then was also in Charlene?

I began to seek God for answers. Charlene was always in a horrible mood after I spent an evening in prayer. God showed me through Scripture that I was dealing with a woman who had an evil spirit. Charlene's desire for power, her use of anger, her rebellion and jealousy had given demonic forces legal ground in her life. Sin had overpowered her and consumed her behavior as she played out the evil of the spirit of Jezebel.

Even though they refused to be my friends, the other women could see a difference in our lives as we worked side by side. One astute typist mentioned, "We can see what is going on between Diane and Charlene; it is a battle between good and evil, God and Satan!" They saw how Charlene was purposely making my life miserable because I refused to cater to her. I was a threat because her failure to control me was an embarrassment. Perhaps her personal power wasn't so great after all! Charlene thought she owned the others in the office. Seeing me resist her might give the others the idea to resist her control. I was also a threat because I had the message of freedom from sin with the gospel of Jesus Christ. Given the opportunity, I was ready to share this message of freedom with the others.

One time she was leaving for the day, but before she left she turned and glared at me. As I looked at her face, her eyes were filled with fiery hatred. "I will finish you off!" I heard a voice speak to my mind, disclosing its vow. Later on I heard the voice of God say to me, "You have a mortal enemy!" God wanted me to know that my situation was serious and that I had to be careful. As I continued to pray, He gave me several dreams to show me that I was on the right track.

In one dream I saw a huge face of a woman in the sky. She was very beautiful; her skin was polished and flawless. I could see her painted lips moving as she called out to people. "Come to me! Come to me! I love you! I love you!" Then, with no change in expression she mouthed these words, "I hate you people of earth, and I want you dead!" It was a vision of the spirit of Jezebel. I continued for months to pray against her power, sometimes three or four nights per week. Several times God called me to pray all night long.

Still, the presence of evil in that office was very strong. I began to have chest pains from the stress and often cried at night from feeling so hated. The stakes became very high involving my job, my health, and even my faith. One time I considered quitting my job. "I don't have to take this!" I thought to myself. "I'll get another job." But God firmly warned me, "If you leave—you lose!" For some reason, this battle was very important, yet being in her presence was painful and difficult.

Three times I told God that it hurt too much to be a Christian anymore. I stopped praying and reading my Bible for a few days. When I picked up my Bible to read again, the Holy Spirit whispered to me, "Diane, my words are life to you!" If I put down my Bible, I would cut off His communication to talk me through the battle. So I continued to hold on to God's promises: **"Do not gloat over me my enemy! Though I have fallen, I will rise. Though I sit in darkness, the Lord is my light…He will bring me out. I will see his righteousness…she who said to me 'Where is the Lord your God?' My eyes will see her downfall; even now she will be trampled underfoot like mire in the streets." (Micah 7:8-10 NIV)**

After eleven months, God gave me another dream to show me that I had won the prayer battle. The spirit of Jezebel's power had been broken. In the dream He showed me a table with witnesses seated around it. I sat on one side and Charlene sat across from me. She was signing a document, like surrender papers, formally conceding to me. The next day when I went into the office Charlene was very sedate, so I knew that the dream was true. A few months later Charlene quit her job. She had become so preoccupied with her drinking and her control measures that she was doing poorly at work. She fled the company for fear of being fired herself!

GOD'S LESSON FOR ME

The spirit of Jezebel is an evil spirit that invades people's lives, but we cannot play innocent by saying, "The devil made me do it!" Despite strong spiritual influences, we are still responsible for our own behavior. That is why we need to see the evil within us that causes us to act the way we do.

Looking back, I could see how God used this time of intense prayer to show me the true condition of my own heart. In the heat of circumstances, everything came into full view—my fear, my pride, my anger, my self-sufficiency. I was repulsed by what I saw in Charlene—her hating, her lying schemes and control tactics. I hated those ways enough to confess and repent of them myself. Her evil was magnified before me so that I might understand the awfulness of my own sin. This was the only way I could feel sin's pain and realize the harm it does. This battle was God's way to lead me in repentance.

At the photography studio, I had vowed to get as far away from evil as possible. Now God was helping me fulfill that vow. In this life, the only way I could distance myself from the presence of evil was through personal repentance and surrender to the supremacy of Christ.

In Scripture, Jezebel's reign of power was short-lived. Jehu had been anointed by the prophet Elisha to be the next king of Israel, displacing Ahab and de-throning Jezebel. As he rode into Jezreel, he looked up and saw Jezebel taunting him from an upper window. Several eunuchs appeared at the window with her. Jehu called out to them, **"Throw her down!" (2 Kings 9:33 NIV)** They took his side against her and threw her down. For me, the window represented an opportunity for me to see Jezebel full view in the life of Charlene. The eunuchs overpowered Jezebel simply by obeying God's Word personally spoken to them. Although I was powerless on my own, with the power of Christ I was able to do the same.

Now I can put a name on the shadowy woman I had seen so many years ago. She had been an apparition, a mysterious, unidentified, yet real evil presence. Back then, I could only see her faintly, but with God's wisdom, today I can distinguish her fully. I understand this pattern of behavior when I see it in others. I know what she is all about. By resisting her and repenting of her ways I was able to personally de-throne the Queen. Seeing Jezebel, I had seen the truth of who I really was because "she" was also in me.

PART III

TRUE CORONATION

∽ Chapter 14 ∽
REPENTANCE

Realizing the depth of my need of God was to my advantage. I found that emptying my container of the many sin barriers was the key to relief from my depression. Besides the benefit of my personal healing, another reason for my cleansing was to make me useful to help others. "**If a man cleanses himself from the latter he will be an instrument for noble purposes, made holy, useful to the master and prepared to do any good work." (2 Timothy 2:21 NIV)**

DYING

God showed me that the only way a Christian can really be useful is if he "dies." **"Unless a kernel of wheat falls to the ground and dies, it remains only a single seed. But if it dies, it produces many seeds." (John 12:24 NIV)** This is figurative language that pictures the Christian life as a single grain of wheat. It signifies a person willing to give up sin, the worship of self, give up what he wants and expects out of life, give up his rights and opinions to fully release himself to God for the sake of the Gospel.

God promises that something wonderful transpires spiritually when a Christian goes deep beneath the surface to "die." The hard, outer covering of self falls away and, by God's power, the Person of Jesus Christ rises up to express Himself through the human personality. By dying, that person can be transformed to be like Jesus.

After all I had seen about myself, I wanted this change and knew that it would be worth dying for.

A CHANGE OF MIND

One of the main Christian disciplines mentioned in Scripture that accomplishes the work of dying in us is repentance. Through the basic practices of Bible reading and prayer, we become aware of inner attitudes that we see are wrong. As if approaching two paths going in opposite directions, the heart comes to a crisis point when we clearly distinguish how we have been living versus how God wants us to live. We must make a conscious decision to either let sin have its way or turn away from it to let God have His way.

Repentance, then, is changing our mind about what we are doing. By saying "no" to sin, we let go of its misleading hand to turn and walk in right fellowship with God. This change of direction in the mind and heart will result in a changed life. Transformation will gradually, yet marvelously take place!

Our motive for repentance is to draw closer to a fearfully holy, yet wonderfully personal God. We are compelled by love to quit sin habits that are repulsive to Him. We take such joy in our reconciliation that we permit nothing to come between us and our Savior.

Repentance is an absorbing desire for God's cleansing; a life once bathed in divine forgiveness, coming again and again to those living waters to be renewed. We choose to come out from under the rule of the sinful nature to enjoy the freedom in God's holy nature. No more hiding in the shadows. We step out to live in the light. Furthermore, it is the heart of the obedient child rising upward to seek the pleasure of the Father by wanting to get totally right with Him. Most importantly, it is the adoring worshipper accepting God's intentions for him and submitting himself to the supremacy of Christ.

CONVICTION

The key to our repentance is our cooperation with the Holy Spirit as He visits us with conviction. Only the Spirit of Christ knows what has yet to come under His lordship. Conviction is God voicing a grief or complaint to the heart about a specific sin. The truth is made known to us so that we will understand our error. If we take the correction, we admit the sin to God and to ourselves. In this way, the Spirit leads us out of self-deception to live honestly before God. But if we believe our own good reasons for sin instead, we block the change that God wants to bring about.

A message by a young pastor illustrates how God brings conviction as we seek Him. He told of a visit to see his grandmother. As he spent time with her, she became tired and went to bed early. He laid down on the couch and began to commune with God.

"Oh God," he prayed, "Please show me what still remains in me that is not pleasing to you." Within the hour he was reminded of a situation in which he was deeply hurt. Before he could dwell on the offense, God spoke to him.

"The pain that is in your heart right now you are causing other people." God's conviction made him reconsider the way he was treating others. A closer look at God will always mean a closer look at ourselves and a decision to change.

TAKING OUT THE GARBAGE

God continually works to bring us to such decision points, making repentance an ongoing process. He brings power to empty out of our container those things that are not of Him. Repentance is "taking out the garbage," the removal of falsehood, stains, wrinkles, and legal ground that have accumulated in us.

Once we have been emptied out, we can enjoy the Spirit's infilling. The purpose of repentance is to refresh the Church with a greater presence of the Holy Spirit. The floodgates of Heaven are opened when sin barriers are removed, allowing the river of God's presence to freely flow. **"Repent, then, and turn to God, so that your sins may be wiped out, that times of refreshing may come from the Lord, who has been appointed for you—even Jesus." (Acts 3:19 NIV)** The supremacy of Christ is accompanied by the presence of Christ, both for the Church and for the individual. When we earnestly seek Him, He will be found by us.

JOSEPH GOD'S VESSEL OF GRACE

One of the best dramas of repentance is seen in the events leading up to the reunion of Joseph and his family. This story represents Christ sharing Himself with us through revelation once the sin barriers are removed.

Joseph's brothers sold him into slavery as a youth because they envied him as his father's favorite. Joseph was taken to Egypt and was sold again to serve under Pharaoh. Eventually, he was raised to power as second in command of Egypt.

Years later, Joseph's brothers traveled to Egypt to purchase food because the famine in Canaan was severe. They presented themselves to Joseph, but did not recognize him as their brother. Joseph longs to reunite with his family, but decides to first deal with the family interpersonal problems before revealing his identity.

Before he sent the brothers back to Canaan, Joseph gave these instructions to his steward, **"Fill the men's sacks with as much food as they can carry and put each man's silver in the mouth of his sack. Then put my cup, the silver one, in the mouth of the youngest one's sack, along with the silver for his grain." (Genesis 44:1-2 NIV)** Joseph pinpointed the cause of strife between them. The silver cup represented God placing His finger on the issue of favoritism, the root cause of competition, jealousy, and strife for three generations. It began with the out-maneuvering between Jacob and Esau, the conflict between Rachael and Leah, and the attempted murder of Joseph by his brothers. It was time to end this generational sin.

In the next part of the plan, Joseph said to the steward, **"Go after those men at once, and when you catch up with them, say to them. 'Why have you repaid good with evil? Isn't this the cup my master drinks from and also uses for divination? This is a wicked thing you have done!'" (Genesis 44:4-5 NIV)** This was the voice of conviction going forth from the mouth of God speaking to their hearts about sin.

The brothers had long buried the memory of their sin against Joseph. When questioned about the cup, they pleaded innocent. **"Why does my Lord say such things? Far be it from your servants to do anything like that!" (Genesis 44:7 NIV)** The brothers were defending themselves with basically good thinking. "We are such good people! We would never do anything like that!" We can sense the wrestling match going on between man's reasoning and God's conviction.

They offered themselves to be searched, not expecting anything to be found. But when their packs were opened, the cup was found with Benjamin. This is a picture of the Holy Spirit exposing truth to the heart. Self-justification permeates our thinking so much that we have trouble believing the wrong we have actually done. As God shows us our secret sins, unbelief is confronted by truth. Then we have a choice to go on believing our own flawed reasoning or accept the truth.

The trip back to answer to Joseph was undoubtedly a long, quiet ride. The brothers had time to think about their lives and consider their sin. By appearances, they had been caught stealing the silver cup and then lying about it. This meant certain death for all of them. With their hearts in utter crisis, they finally turned to the truth.

As they faced Joseph, Judah abandoned all self-defense. **"What can we say to my Lord?...God has uncovered your servant's guilt." (Genesis 44:16 NIV)** Then he went on to tell their long-kept secret of selling their brother into slavery. The purpose of Joseph's search was to bring enough pressure on the brothers to let them feel the weight of their sin and confess it.

Joseph could no longer control himself as he wept over the complications that sin had caused: his own imprisonment, his brother's years of living with guilt, his father's pain of losing a son, and all the separation the family members had suffered. God's heart aches over the unnecessary ravages of sin.

Then Joseph revealed his true identity to his brothers. **"But his brothers were not able to answer him, because they were terrified at his presence. Then Joseph said to his brothers, 'Come close to me.'"(Genesis 45:3-4 NIV)** The revealed holiness of God is terrifying to the darkened heart. Yet God portions out His truth in bearable amounts because He wants us to come near to Him. After the brothers made their confession, Joseph extended forgiveness. Likewise, God expects the full truth from us because He is willing to give a full pardon. This means that we are released from sin's guilt and have peace in our conscience.

It was the combination of grace and truth that exposed the sin issues of this family, bringing sweet reconciliation among brothers and revival to their father's heart. This is the nature of Jesus that was celebrated by the early disciples, **"We have seen his glory, the glory of the one and only son, who came from the Father, full of grace and truth." (John 1:14 NIV)**

The purpose of repentance is not to rub our nose in our sin, but to bring relief from sin's oppression. The Holy Spirit wants to help us resolve our personal conflicts, revive us with hope, and restore us to a close fellowship with God. He wants the rule of Jesus Christ to bear upon us rather than the load of guilt from unconfessed sin.

Jesus is full of grace and truth. This means that a deep, thorough spiritual cleansing is possible for every believer. God is willing to show us as much of ourselves as we agree to see. We learn to value God's grace as we are exposed to His truth. His hand of mercy breaks the fall of exalted self deposed. But the exciting part of repentance is that we also experience a new measure of Christ as, by grace, His truth takes its secret place inside of us. This is how we draw close to Him.

∾ Chapter 15 ∾
LOVING GOD

L oving God is our utmost reason for repentance, worship, or any other type of Christian service. When we fall in love with Jesus, we are powerfully moved to shift our focus off of ourselves and onto Him. Our love for Him overrides our love of self. Then we begin to live a self-sacrificial life for His sake. **"...and they loved not their lives unto the death." (Revelation 12:11 KJV)** Without a deeply imbedded, underlying love for the Person of Christ, our faith in Him is flat and unfeeling.

Loving God is merely love returned. **"We love because He first loved us." (1 John 4:19 NAS)** Our love of Jesus swells from an inner gratitude for the love He expressed when He laid down his life for us. Our adoration of our Heavenly Father stems from an appreciation of the unmerited rescue from death and subsequent new life He gives us in Christ.

JESUS OUR RESCUER
Salvation is preservation from destruction. It involves the life-saving action of a stronger, firmly secured party considering the need of a helpless, ill-fated victim and then moving to perform a rescue. This was Christ's role as Savior when He came to earth, lived as a Man, and suffered the penalty of sin on our behalf. His intervention preserves all who believe from God's judgment. His abiding presence protects those who are His. **"My prayer is not that you**

take them out of the world but that you protect them from the evil one." (John 17:15 NIV)

For example, the Father performed a remarkable rescue for a friend of mine when she was making plans to adopt a baby from India. The baby had been aborted by an unwed Hindu girl who had gone to a nursing home for the procedure seven months into the pregnancy. Weighing only 2 lb. 3 oz., little Mithu was born alive and whole. She was left alone to survive her first night with no care. By a miracle, she lived and was claimed by some nurses from a Missions organization the next day. After her health stabilized, Mithu was adopted by my friend who was able to give her a new life in America.

This speaks of our spiritual condition before we were "born-again." Just like little Mithu, without Christ we were helpless, struggling, and without hope. At the moment we believed, God spoke to our hearts saying, "You are mine! Come with Me and live!" With saving power, we were rescued from death and made alive to God. Thus, we were adopted into God's family and received the benefits of being called "children of God." Understanding all that God has done to save us from our peril should give us tremendous cause to love Him.

LOVE TOOK HOLD

Our conversion was the entrance point of real love. When Jesus came into our lives, Love's power took hold of us. To imagine that the immeasurable God would dote on our affections for Him is incomprehensible. Yet He thrills at the faintest echo of returned love from the heart chambers of regenerate man. **"You have stolen my heart, my sister, my bride, you have stolen my heart with one glance of your eyes…" (Song of Songs 4:9 NIV)** If we relish His love, we can never count it too much to be tender towards Him. We should be willing to meet His desire for us with all the love we have to give.

We need to value our relationship with Jesus above all else. His demonstration of love was expensive for Him. We should hold Him near and dear, much like a married woman to her husband. **"This is a profound mystery—but I am talking about Christ and the Church. However each one of you must love his wife as he loves himself, and the wife must respect her husband..." (Ephesians 5:32-33 NIV)**

We must be careful not to fall into the trap of accepting the world's concept of marriage, where pledging oneself to another and the finality of the covenant has been greatly subverted. In the world, people often question the value of staying together when the personal benefits diminish. We see a parody of modern marriage in the 1970's film "The Heartbreak Kid." Richard Groden finally finds the girl of his dreams while on vacation in Florida. He becomes crazed over a coy, manipulating co-ed played by Sybil Shepherd. Unfortunately, the timing is poor, he admits, because he is on his honeymoon. Oops!

We watch as he extricates himself from his new, but less desirable marriage, and worms his way into the life of his dream-girl. Sybil is plainly bored with him but finally marries him, giving in to his selfish persistence. What seemed ridiculously funny years ago is not far from the truth about marriage relationships today.

As Christians, we dare not adopt this same self-serving attitude towards Christ. We cannot decide what we want, snap our fingers, and expect Christ to come running more on the order of milady and her butler than a husband and his adoring bride. Even worse, we cannot allow our hearts to wander, entertaining the notion of having something better when Christianity doesn't seem to work for us. Our faithfulness to Christ is a key indicator of our undying love for Him.

LOVING GOD THROUGH OBEDIENCE

Bowing our will to the revealed will of God is the best way we can show our love to Him. Our love is played out by obeying what God tells us to do. **"If you love me, you will obey what I command." (John 14:15 NIV)** We purpose in our hearts to say "Yes" to Him as He makes His requests known.

Many times during our daily Bible reading, God will give us directives to obey. He may give guidance on how to handle a specific problem or challenge us to change a certain behavior. When God personalizes a verse, something illuminates inside us as we read. When that happens, we need to believe that God is speaking to us and pay attention to what He says.

Regardless of how our human reasoning argues or finds excuses, we need to override the protests of the flesh and act upon those spiritual words. We will find that **"his commands are not burdensome." (1 John 5:3 NIV)** and are for our good. Over time, we will discover that we were wise to obey every request.

LOVING GOD THROUGH REPENTANCE

God will especially speak to us about our specific sin. Out of loving regard for Him, our response to conviction should be repentance. Many times I have heard people vocalize the exact sin that God has been speaking to them about. There was no question in their mind about what God had said. Yet their decision to obey was halted by their reason for wanting the sin. In this case, love for God had not won over the love of sin and self.

The sinful woman mentioned in Luke 7 did not defend her reasons for sin. Instead, she obeyed as the Spirit led her in a humiliating display of public repentance. **"When a woman who had lived a sinful life in that town learned that Jesus was eating at the Pharisee's house, she brought an alabaster jar of perfume and as she stood behind him at his feet weeping, she began to wet his feet with her tears. Then she wiped them with her hair, kissed them and poured perfume on them." (Luke 7:37-38 NIV)**

This woman was distraught over her sin. She pursued Jesus for His forgiveness, even if it meant facing a room full of judgmental Pharisees. The Pharisees also led sinful lives in different ways. But their hearts were so guarded with proud reasoning that conviction did not touch them.

So Jesus allowed a display of abandoned repentance to show them, and us, how to give it up and melt at His feet when

He speaks to us about sin. That woman who mournfully despised all the wrong she had done fell more deeply in love with Jesus as He pardoned her and dismissed her in peace. **"Therefore, I tell you, her many sins have been forgiven—for she loved much. But he who has been forgiven little loves little." (Luke 7:47 NIV)** Repentance, then, is our opportunity to experience an even greater measure of God's love. As we openly confess sin to God, we can know His forgiveness and be released to love Him all the more for it.

LOVING GOD THROUGH GODLY LIVING

Another way we can express our love for God is by honoring Him with godly living. When we remind ourselves that we live in full view of God, we will want to have a good conscience towards Him. **"May the words of my mouth and the meditation of my heart be pleasing in your sight, O Lord, my Rock and my Redeemer." (Psalm 19:14 NIV)** When faced with the demands of the day, we choose to live in a way that pleases God, regardless if we are commended for it. We hold to righteous living because we look forward to facing Jesus some day. Our love for Him forbids us to cause Him any disappointment.

Because we are living for a future glory, we need to have an attitude of separation now. This mindset says, "I see other people doing things which God has shown me are wrong. Even though these people are my friends, their actions are not for me. Because I love God, I want to live for Him." Choosing to pull away from ungodly behavior shows how serious we are about our True Love.

One behavior we need to be separated from unless married is immoral sexual activity. **"For this is the will of God, your sanctification; that each one of you know how to control your own body in holiness and honor, not with lustful passion, like the Gentiles who do not know God." (1 Thessalonians 4:3-5 NIV)** Scripture is clear that having sex outside of marriage is wrong. Furthermore, we are not to entice others with our hair, eyes or bodies to get attention for ourselves. That includes mind games, flirtation, suggestive body language, provocative speech, or anything else which might tease or lead to fornication.

If we are having sexual encounters without being married or married but being unfaithful, we need to ask for God's strength and wisdom to extricate ourselves from that situation. If our desire is to get right with God, He will make a way for us to do that. If we are single and being tempted or getting pressure from a man who says he loves us, then we need to question his walk with Christ and re-evaluate that relationship. It is important for our own well-being to take a strong stand in this area. God calls us to a life of purity regardless if a man is calling us to bed.

LOVING GOD THROUGH TESTING

Often we have times of testing to prove our love for Christ. It is God's preference to choose the time and method by which He tests the hearts of his sons and daughters. Thus He opens our lives as a display before God and man. **"The crucible for silver and the furnace for gold but the Lord tests the heart." (Proverbs 17:3 NIV)** Our love will be found true, genuine, and pure when we love God even during hardship.

The Lord is mainly interested in what comes forth from a life under pressure. How we respond to difficulties quickly reveals the true matters of the heart. God seeks the answers to two questions through testing: Do we love God only for His blessing? And what are we like when we don't get our own way?

I was recently inspired as to the answers to those questions by the label on the back of a package of potpourri. "Heavenly aromas will fill your home within minutes as this potpourri of air freshening herbs, fruit peels, and spices gently simmer on the stove." The thought of heavenly aromas filling a room was wonderfully appealing. But for that to happen, those ingredients must be dried, mixed together, and then crushed before they can simmer over a flame to release their fragrance. This marvelous scent takes on a much more precious meaning when the drying, mixing, and crushing are brought into the context of the Christian life.

The same two questions were put forth when Satan petitioned God for Job's life. His purpose was to disprove Job's love of God through hardship. **"'Does Job fear God for nothing?' Satan replied. 'Have you not put a hedge around him and his household and everything he has? You have blessed the works of his hands...But stretch out your hand and strike everything he has, and he will surely curse you to your face.' The Lord said to Satan, 'Very well, then, everything he has is in your hands but on the man himself do not lay a finger.'" (Job 1:9-12 NIV)**

Satan soon had his way. When the dust settled over Job and his wife, their bout with spiritual testing ended in multiple tragedies. But there were two distinctly different aromas that arose from the ashes of their lives. As we come close to the scene and take a whiff, we cannot help but wrinkle our nose at the strong odor coming from Job's wife. **"Curse God and die!" (Job 2:9 NIV)** Her response to hardship was not only to withdraw her love from God, but also from her husband in angry blame. Satan proved his point with her.

Meanwhile, Job's mind was reeling as he searched for some explanation that would comfort him. Nonetheless, the essence of his heart seeped out. **"Shall we accept good from God and not trouble?...Though he slay me, yet I will hope in him." (Job 2:10, Job 13:15 NIV)** His answer proved that, even through the bitterest trials, we can draw a weary breath to blow a kiss to Christ, thus filling Heaven's throne room with fragrant love coming forth from our life.

This was the "potpourri" that simmered in the life of a friend as she went through her own portion of Job circumstances. This was a woman I worked with who had eight children, including a six month old baby. When tragedy struck, the true motives of her heart were on display before God and man. The family had been out shopping and when they came home they found the fire department putting out the final blazes that had consumed their house. Fortunately, the family had been away and no one was hurt, but they lost all their household belongings in the fire.

I heard about the bad news and expected my friend to be a nervous wreck when she came back to work. Instead, she had a calm smile on her face and a sparkle in her eyes.

"We still have our family," she explained. "Everything else can be replaced! God is so good!"

Love that flows during trying times like these are very special sacrifices to God. **"Then make an offering by fire to the Lord, a burnt offering or sacrifice...to make a soothing aroma to the Lord." (Numbers 15:3 NAS)** When we choose to exalt Christ because we believe His goodness is far beyond our crumbling circumstances, then our love is proven by our faith in Him. We show that we prefer our treasure in Heaven over our earthly treasure and He is that heavenly treasure!

LOVING GOD THROUGH SERVANTHOOD

This leads us to loving God through servant hood. God equates our serving others directly with serving Him. **"Whatever you did for the least of these brothers of mine, you did for me." (Matthew 25:40 NIV)** We are doing what He would do if He were physically here.

Serving God includes, yet goes beyond the basics of church-going, Bible study, and prayer. God will show us the good works He has mapped out for us on our journey in Christ. **"For we are God's workmanship, created in Christ Jesus to do good works, which God prepared in advance for us to do." (Ephesians 2:10 NIV)** God has prepared a destiny for each of us. The key to walking in that destiny is in following Christ closely. Our good works are hidden in Him. In order to do the good which God has intended, we must seek Christ and He will give us the next step.

The servant is literally at the Master's beck and call any hour, any place, any request. **"Whoever serves me must follow me; and where I am, my servant also will be." (John 12:26 NIV)** Active servant hood will lay claim to our spare time, our not-so spare time, our money, our relationships, and all other activities. The Master wants to redeem all of these resources for His use.

The benefit to us as servants is that God's good works have a way of doing an equally good work in us. Because God's work is spiritual, the divine nature in us must override the self nature to accomplish the task we have been given. A change occurs as we put off self and allow God's power to take over. As we practice servant hood, new ground is taken in us for Christ. Doing the works of Jesus by Jesus' power helps us towards Christ's supremacy.

Unbelievers will recognize the work of the servant as being from God because it is distinctly and impossibly unselfish. God reaches out to people using willing, obedient servants, breaking through to them with works of godly love. **"It was I who healed them. I led them with cords of human kindness, with ties of love." (Hosea 11:4 NIV)** All God needs is a warm body with a warm heart towards Him, and He will do the rest to reconcile the world to Himself.

Some of the greatest serving we can do is to offer what we have learned from our own suffering. People need their troubles explained to them in Biblical terms. What better service than to offer the wisdom necessary to help people climb out of their difficulties. Our lives can become an example of hope for others, turning our personal misery into our personal ministry! **"Therefore, I am now going to allure her; I will lead her into the desert and speak tenderly to her. There I will give her back her vineyards and will make the Valley of Achor a door of hope." (Hosea 2:14-15 NIV)** When we go through painful times, God has our attention and speaks to us, showing us truths of which we were ignorant. In the Valley of Trouble, we learn to value Christ as our only way out. As He restores us, we are impacted and convinced to urge others to find their help in Christ.

We discover our usefulness as He brings people who can relate to our past places of trouble. Our lives become open doors for others to walk through to find their answers. Serving God in a hurting world is an expression of love that puts a sparkle in a servant's eyes and a "Yes" continually on his lips. At our own sweet expense, we can savor life's purpose as we do the works of Jesus out of love for Him.

∞ Chapter 16 ∞
HUMILITY

The arch rival for our affections with which we love God is our love of self. Self competes for attention, credit, admiration, and renown that belongs to God. We cannot promote both self and God. At our own expense, we must decide to stand back and let Him receive all the glory. **"He must increase, but I must decrease."** **(John 3:30 KJV)** We cannot be useful if we compete with God, craving what is rightfully His.

Humility, then, is the voluntary death of our own self-importance. It is the process of shrinking the size of self in our minds as we consider the Biblical size of God. The more we understand His numerous attributes and unequaled power, the more we step down from our admiration of self. Humility bids us to leave our self-loyalty, much like defecting to another country to go live in a greater land.

The discipline of humility involves a rigorous self-inspection, intent on discovering one's own fallen ways. If we are willing to question our own prideful image, then God will show us true self in the light of Christ. The Apostle Paul experienced his own personal comparison with Christ. Consequently, he backed down from being a self-righteous zealot to being a man who insisted, **"Here is a trustworthy saying that deserves full acceptance: Jesus Christ came into the world to save sinners—of whom I am the worst."** **(1 Timothy 1:15 NIV)** We would do well to invite the Holy Spirit to pull back the veil of self and expose who is behind the image we are projecting.

139

Humility is also the transfer of trust in ourselves to trust in God. Like bank funds, we withdraw from the "self account" to make a faith deposit in the "God account." Andrew Murray describes humility as "the place of entire dependence on God."[31] Our state of bankruptcy in self needs to become apparent so that we will want to attain a new level of dependence on God.

We also need to personally reclaim Heaven's view which sees God as the source of all we are and all we do. To dwell in the reality that our very existence hinges on Christ helps keep our haughty attitudes in check. We are merely recipients of God's liberal sharing. **"What do you have that you did not receive? And if you did receive it, why do you boast as though you did not?" (1 Corinthians 4:7 NIV)** A spirit of humility boasts about God and credits nothing to self.

I CAN'T BUT GOD CAN

God had a work of humility in mind when He let Joseph waste away in prison for two years. For this man to be useful to God, he had to be cured of any vain reasoning that would ascribe personal power to himself. Joseph had a lot going for him in the natural. But he had to see that his youthful strength, leadership talent, and good looks were not a means of power for him. Otherwise, the temptation to misuse God's power would be too great. During those two silent years Joseph must have transferred all his trust from the "self account" to the "God account", placing his hope for deliverance from prison in God's power alone.

The evidence of humility came when Pharaoh asked Joseph to interpret a dream. **"'I cannot do it,' Joseph replied to Pharaoh, 'but God will give Pharaoh the answer he desires.'" (Genesis 41:16 NIV)** "I can't, but God can!" confesses the humble at heart. The discipline of humility converts us from "Awe shucks!" to silent, reverent "Awe!"

Pharaoh received his answer from God and was pleased to put Joseph in charge of the whole land of Egypt. A person who is suffi-

---

31 Humility, p. 10

ciently humbled is the only kind God can trust to steward a position of true power and authority. That person will act as God's agent rather than an agent for himself. He will see the saving good which comes as completely God's doing rather than giving credit to self. And he will keep Heaven's insight by seeing God as the only source of goodness, wisdom, power, and glory as he humbly relies on Him.

DESPERATION

We would be most successfully humbled if our dependency gave way to desperation for God. Then we would see life as a fragile, single strand thread and would marvel at how we are sustained from above. The flesh may squirm at the thought of reaching this extreme level of weakness. But as we humble ourselves, we become deaf-eared to the protests of the flesh and cry out to God with genuine felt necessity. **"I hear a cry of a woman in labor, a groan as if one bearing her first born son—the cry of the Daughter of Zion gasping for breath." (Jeremiah 4:31 NIV)**

In desperation, we would be so diminished in our own view that we would turn to prayer as a life essential. As if breathing via life support equipment, we would feel the urgency to inhale a fresh supply of God's presence. Our inner being would plead for His entrance, "Oh, God, how I need you!"

To learn about humility is one matter, but to learn humility through experience is quite another. There is a life-altering difference between learning truth and living truth. One difficult winter I felt depleted and desperate for God. The wind chill had nudged the temperature well below zero, draining the last glimmer of charge out of my car battery. As I sat motionless, staring at my car, waiting for my dad to come with jumper cables, the Lord spoke to me ever so gently, "That's you." He brought to mind the drained, wind-blown battery along with this verse, **"I am the vine, you are the branches…apart from me you can do nothing." (John 15:5 NIV)** The lesson of humility was imbedded in me through the experience of desperation. I needed to be humbled by this truth to help me grow in the assurance of God's power alone.

GODLY SORROW

Truth humbles us and the One who guides us in all truth is the Person of the Holy Spirit. Humility and repentance come only as we seek His aid to show us our sin. Otherwise, we are much too biased towards self to bring sufficient scrutiny to our own lives. Sin is so interwoven into our thinking that we cannot possible discern it all, nor can we imagine the vastness of our sinful state. Oswald Chambers comments about the movement of the Spirit as He searches us. "The great mystical work of the Holy Spirit is in the dim regions of our personality which we cannot get at."[32] Rather than decide for ourselves, we need to let God make His own determination of the ills of our soul.

Just as a river cannot be grasped by human hands, so we cannot guess or control the course of the Holy Spirit as He deals with us. One thing we do know is that we are dealing with Power! As we present ourselves to God, we should anticipate His conviction to come with His presence. We will experience godly sorrow as His truth pierces us. Godly sorrow is the emotion that comes when a person feels bad about his sin and grieves over his offenses. The emotions respond to the inner realization of doing wrong. This is the Holy Spirit's work of plowing up the soil of the heart, breaking up the hardness of sin and self. Tears are a physical sign of the heart being flushed out of its independent, foolish ways. There is an aspect of coming near to God which causes man to come unpleasantly apart at the seams. **"Come near to God and he will come near to you. Wash your hands, you sinners, and purify your hearts, you double-minded. Grieve, mourn and wail. Change your laughter to mourning and your joy to gloom. Humble yourselves before the Lord, and he will lift you up." (James 4:8-10 NIV)** Crying during our repentance should become normal. If we know to expect it, then we won't resist it.

Don't Worry—Be Happy

Too many times we refuse to cry because of embarrassment. We hold ourselves back because it is an affront to our ability to stay

32   My Utmost For His Highest, p. 6

in control. It is too messy and uncool. Rather than get too shook up, we prefer to remain strong, stoic, and therefore, unmoved.

The problem in our culture is that feeling bad about doing wrong is not popular. Our "Positive Thinking" teachers have trained us to override the inner pleadings, insisting on feeling good, staying up, and being positive. Their doctrine is reinforced by modern idioms such as "Don't worry! Be happy!" and the indelible grin of the yellow "Smiley Face."

For example, one day I walked past two friends who were parting company on the sidewalk. I heard their final remarks about how they were really feeling their age. One of the men smiled proudly as he advised his friend, "As long as we are having a good time, that's all that counts!"

We insulate ourselves with feel good attitudes to make sure that nothing bothers us. That way, self can remain untouched. The Bible comments on this disposition. **"He says to himself, 'Nothing will shake me; I'll always be happy and never have trouble.'" (Psalm 10:6 NIV)** We refuse to feel the discomfort of facing the reality of our condition. So we put on a happy face and pretend everything is fine, even though we know it isn't. As we steel ourselves to refuse to feel bad about the mess that sin has made, stoic pride resists the Spirit's breaking power.

Godly Sorrow Is a Deterrent

God wants to move people to grief because godly sorrow is a deterrent to sin. Like an impression made in soft plaster, the wrong of sin impacts us so that, when the tears dry, we will not want to sin that way again. The Holy Spirit allows us to experience the full weight of our sin so that we will understand its seriousness. God wants us to hate the sin once we see it and then feel remorse for what we've done. **"There you will remember your conduct and all your actions by which you have defiled yourselves and you will loathe yourselves for what you have done." (Ezekiel 20: 43 NIV)** When our conscience is stricken by truth, we suffer pain in our emotions. The pain of sin then outweighs the pleasure of sin. This is the turning point when we decide to change our ways. Like a spanking to the backside, so God deals with us in our heart.

Grieving Loss

The Spirit may also lead us to grieve over loss we have suffered to relieve us from pain we are carrying. **"Come to Me, all who are weary and heavy-laden, and I will give you rest." (Matthew 11:28 NAS)** The loss of loved ones from either death or divorce especially affects us. For example, soon after becoming a Christian, a friend began to experience the cleansing work of the Holy Spirit. She was strongly moved to grieve the death of her mother which had occurred when she was three years old. I explained that God was working to remove that burden of sadness from her. She had been too young to know how to express herself at the time of the loss.

We need to be real with God about our distress. We can admit, "God, these things really bother me! I'm hurting! Please help me where I hurt!" He already knows, but needs our cooperation to take us through the grief. Someday in Heaven every tear will be wiped away. But until then, the tears need to flow as we get in touch with the reality of how sin has harmed us.

HEALED MEMORIES

There are several ways that the Spirit will point out the areas He is calling us to repentance. One way is by allowing circumstances to build, bringing us under a degree of pressure that forces sin to surface. This exposure of our sin is compared to silver refining. **"On that day a fountain will be opened to the house of David and the inhabitants of Jerusalem, to cleanse them from sin and impurity...This third I will bring into the fire; I will refine them like silver and test them like gold." (Zechariah 13:1-9 NIV)** As the temperature of the fire rises, the impurities surface on the molten metal and are skimmed off by the refiner.

In the same way, as life's pressures build, unresolved conflicts and sin issues will fester within us. We may have memory flashbacks of painful times. Our past will come into sudden view when triggered by a similar event while under pressure. Then we can see the source of our sin, repent, and be fully cleansed. I remember discovering intense feelings of anger while going through the crisis of unemployment. I asked God to show me the cause, and He reminded me of entrance points for my angry reactions. I was able to resolve those past offenses through sorrow and forgiveness.

The best example of someone reviewing his life through Spirit guided memory flashbacks is in Charles Dickens story "*A Christmas Carol.*" In the contemporary Muppet version, actor Michael Caine plays the hardened Scrooge who sternly begrudges his best employee, Bob Crachit (Kermit the Frog) a day off for Christmas. As foretold by his deceased partner Joseph Marley, Scrooge is visited on Christmas Eve by the first spirit who transports him to Christmas past. There, Scrooge gets an onlooker's view of himself as a boy.

"Good heavens, it's me!" he gasped, seeing himself alone as an orphan.

Next, he saw the woman he loved and almost married. He realized how badly he hurt her by rejecting her to embrace his greed instead. Now as an old bachelor, he wept as the scene was almost intolerable for him. He had purposely buried the memory beneath the importance of balanced ledgers.

With the next spirit he witnessed his current tyranny of his employees. He saw how his miserly ways caused them to suffer in poverty. The last spirit showed him how the whole town would be relieved if he were dead! By the time the real Christmas came, Scrooge was a broken man, determined to mend his ways. That day he led the whole Muppet town in a song of Christmas praise and thanksgiving!

I can't think of a better picture of how the Spirit of Holiness visits our hearts to give us an onlooker's view of ourselves. As we consider how we have lived, Christ gives us a second chance so that we don't have to be full of regret. He brings us to sorrowful repentance so that we can grieve, and then move on. God is glorified by our transformed lives when people see the difference in us and they can hardly believe it!

MIRROR IMAGE

Another way God humbles us is by using a "mirror" method by bringing us into close contact with someone we feel we can't stand. **"As iron sharpens iron so one man sharpens another." (Proverbs 27:17 NIV)** As the rubbing begins through interaction, that person's faults chafe us. The traits we hate in others may be red flag indicators of problem areas we need to look at honestly within ourselves. We may become irked with our antagonist, but we are actually seeing a display of our own faults as if looking in a mirror.

The Apostle Paul explains this spiritual principle this way, **"…you who pass judgment do the same things." (Romans 2:1 NIV)** This verse has a "boomerang" quality to it. When we toss out a complaint about what someone else is doing, our words have a way of coming back and hooking us with doing the same thing. For instance, there was a time when I couldn't stand a lot of people. I didn't particularly like the conclusion this verse forced me to draw; that I was seeing my own faults. But it was true!

Seeing my mirror image in others and recognizing my true self was a humbling experience. As I endured the rubbing and repented of my sins, my relationships seemed to smooth out as sin lost its power over me.

TIME ALONE WITH GOD

The Spirit deals with us most effectively when we offer Him time alone. Hours spent alone with God allows a deep, deep cleansing that is not possible in a worship service or group Bible study. This verse expresses the importance of having time alone with God: **"The Lord is good to those whose hope is in him; to the one who seeks him; it is good to wait quietly for the salvation of the Lord… Let him sit alone in silence, for the Lord has laid it on him. Let him bury his face in the dust—there may yet be hope." (Lamentations 3:25-29 NIV)** We need to give God time to speak to us, shutting out the distractions that clamor for our attention. He will move on our hearts when we expectantly focus on Him.

The woman at the well had time alone with Jesus. After her encounter, she openly told others, **"Come, see a man who told me everything I ever did." (John 4:29 NIV)** Her time alone with the Savior allowed her to privately reconsider her ways without condemnation. We need to have a heart-to-heart talk with the Man who can tell us everything we ever did. Like a bright, new day after an evening thunderstorm, the hope which lies at the end of godly sorrow is a fresh experience of the saving power of Jesus Christ. Let me share a poem that I wrote one night while spending time alone with God.

My Treasure Vase

Heaven holds a sea of tears
Fed by my life's sad stream.
The wreckage of my past floats by
As memories all too keen.
Deep, salty from the salt-mine tears
That swell my eyelids closed;
Down-buried bedroom pillow tears
Refuse to be exposed;
Barely, blinking, almost tears
A battle bravely fought;
Then streaming down soft cheek-type tears
The end of which there's naught;
Thunderstorm and lightning tears
The kind that burst my soul;
Quaking, shaking, shattering tears
All bound to take their toll;
Desert-dry oasis tears
Though should be there, are gone;
All used up from the heart-sick tears
From draining dreams undone;
Melting, molten lava tears
Deep in the heart are trapped;

All bottled up and fizzing tears
That pops the cork uncapped;
Blurry with confusion tears
That don't know where to land
Then wash up on the shoreline tears
That steal away the sand.
A lifetime of all kinds of tears,
God saves up every one
And strings them on a pearl-like strand
Of dewdrops in the sun.
For each one has its special spot
Inside my treasure vase.
My joy will match my hard-earned wealth
To radiate my face
With tiny, shiny diamond tears
God's precious liquid gems.
Bright, sparkling studded rhinestone tears
When, on Jesus my eyes descend.

Through godly sorrow, we can have God-given light-heartedness and joy when He comes to lift us up. Traveling through grief releases us to walk away free when we reach the other side.

So we must conclude that godly sorrow is one of the many Bible paradoxes that God, in His sovereignty, has chosen to establish: that death would lead to life, humility as God's higher way for us, and Spirit-inspired sorrow would lead to true-felt happiness.

∽ Chapter 17 ∽
CIRCUMVENTING THE CROSS

I was shaken from a night of crying after writing that poem. There was nothing fun about the strain on my emotions that birthed those words. I would have preferred not going through that degree of sorrow, but God did not forewarn me of how He was going to move nor did He ask for my opinion or vote. He knows that the demolition of self is not something that we eagerly stand in line for, waiting to be next. On the contrary, self balks at a personal application of the cross and, with a slew of reasons warns, "Don't go there!"

Certainly there is a price to pay for the transformation which comes from our surrender to Christ's supremacy. That night I learned of the heartache necessary to turn us bland personalities into prophetic poets. So the question that will continually present itself during repentance is, "Are we willing to pay the price?"

The daily decisions we make to put off the voice of self in order to obey Christ are part of the Christian walk known as "the cross." With His own life as the example, Jesus taught about the discipline of dying to do God's will. Jesus said, **"If anyone would come after me, he must deny himself and take up his cross and follow me." (Matthew 16:24 NIV)** At Gethsemane, it was time for Jesus to endure the horror of crucifixion. Jesus was not angry about what was being asked of Him. But He did seek God to see if there was another possible way. **"'Abba Father,' he said, 'everything is possible for you. Take this cup from me. Yet not what I will, but what**

you will.'" (Mark 14:36 NIV) There was no other way for the debt of sin to be paid.

Justice demanded that human sin and self-seeking be punished by death. At the cross, God demonstrated to the utmost His love for us and hatred towards sin. His plan allowed Jesus, the Holy and Righteous One, to become sin and then allowed sin (Jesus) to die. Therefore, the cross was God's perfect will. Jesus chose to obey His Father's will unto death.

At our personal cross, we consciously obey God and refuse sin, thus breaking the self-gratifying hold that sin has upon us. Because our participation in the cross is often painful, inconvenient, unfamiliar, or fearfully life-changing, people find ways to put it off, get around it, or avoid it altogether. D.L. Moody once wrote, "The way to Heaven is straight as a rule, but it is the way of the cross. Don't try to get around it."[33] When we despise the price we must pay to be like the Son, we find reasons to refuse the leading of the Holy Spirit and attempt to circumvent the cross. This is our avoidance of the spiritual discipline of dying. Instead of accepting God's will, we stop short or invent schemes to try to get around what God has said. Ultimately, we are refusing His will to keep our own.

Perhaps we are not fully aware of how we are saying "no" and need to be shown our protective reasoning. The following are some common ways in which we try to circumvent the cross.

BUSY-NESS

Probably the most common way we avoid the cross is through busy-ness. Christian service in the church often adds a new dimension of activity to our schedule. We can easily become busy at church, at home, and with outside commitments. The problem comes when we pile up responsibilities to feel better about ourselves with our accomplishments. When we fill our time to forget or suppress unresolved conflict then, in a sense, we are just stalling.

One of the easiest areas women can hide in busy-ness is in hobbies and crafts. Hobbies can be a sedative to mask pain with crea-

---

33   1100 Illustrations From the Writings of D.L. Moody, p. 107

tive enjoyment or it can be plain self-indulgence. One night I was talking to a lady on the phone who was telling me about all her hobbies.

"I keep myself busy with crafts so that I don't have to think about things." Her voice trailed off as she caught herself in this confession. But she was right. When we get alone and quiet, we begin to think and reflect. This is the perfect atmosphere for the Holy Spirit to speak to our minds. He will help us sort out our thoughts as they surface. But if we are busy thinking about the next thread color, our minds are elsewhere and will escape the Spirit's reach.

God showed me that I was actually stirring Him to jealousy with my hobby of sewing. When I felt depressed and lonely I would head to the fabric store and plan another outfit to sew.

"Every time you feel bad, you run here instead of to Me!" God nabbed me with the truth right in the middle of the store aisle. I was circumventing the cross by trying to find another way to soothe my feelings. God had plans to remove those feelings of depression rather than just put them off.

We need to carefully consider the value of the interests that have captured our time and energies. Are we putting off our own inner healing? Are we active in a role of "Miss Helping Hands" just to show people how nice we are? Or are we spending time with God, seeking Him to better us and make us more effective Christians? The Spirit wants to indwell God's people in the fullest way. We should not put off His work of making room in us. We need to pray about our time schedule so that we will always be in the will of God as He plans our busy days.

HUMAN RELATIONSHIPS

Another way people avoid the cross is through over involvement in other people's lives. Social ties can be emphasized to have such importance that human relationships reign supreme. Family traditions can especially demand our loyal obedience. The rule of family loyalties over following Christ was the issue Jesus addressed when He said, **"If anyone comes to me and does not hate his** father and mother, his wife and children, his brothers and sister—yes, even his own life—he cannot be my disciple." (Luke 14:26 NIV)

Jesus was not speaking against the family unit that He created. He knew how complicated and intertwined family ties can be. Our human sympathies can compete with our relationship to Christ. We can be so involved with others that our time with God is squeezed out. We need to make sure that family is not like god to us. Our relationship with Christ must be above all else.

False Saving

False saving is another behavior which magnifies the importance of human relationships. This can happen two ways. The first is when we become so dependent on other people that we look to them to "save" us. We expect so much life-giving help from others that they become our first resource. It is easier to depend on a human best friend than God who is Spirit. Healthy friendships are wonderful and we certainly need them. But when we automatically turn to spend hours on the phone telling someone our problems and little time in prayer, then we are circumventing the cross. We will maintain unbelief in what God can do if we trust others more than we trust God.

The other extreme is when we busy ourselves with meeting others people's needs. The modern day buzz-word for this people addiction is "codependency." This is when we bury ourselves in others people's problems as a means of feeling important and needed. Slaving for others may seem like a noble cause. But overly-involved rescuing relationships can become ingrown and idolatrous. Our need to be needed can rule our lives as an emotional addiction. Codependency leaves God out because it operates on the strength of human emotions as we rescue and become false saviors of others.

God wants us to focus on Christ, not on the lives of others. **"Let us fix our eyes on Jesus, the author and finisher of our faith…"** **(Hebrews 12:2 NIV)** We need to be sure that our involvement is not a scheme to live vicariously through others, neglecting our own problems and issues, therefore circumventing the cross.

REFUSING THE WORD OF THE LORD

Another way we circumvent the cross is by refusing the Word of the Lord that comes to us. Scripture has demanded action from us that we consider to be too hard or costly. Perhaps God is speaking to us about a certain sin, but we put Him off. "Is there another Word from the Lord?" we ask, "One that does not require so much from me?"

The prophet Jonah ran away from the Word of the Lord after receiving a directive to preach to Nineveh. That word meant doing God's will perhaps at the cost of his own life. The Word of God will always put us in self-sacrificial positions, walking in Christ's footsteps. Yet we scorn the "Ninevehs" where God is showing us. We ignore what we have heard and head in another direction.

The writer of Hebrews wants to bring us back to the cross. **"See to it that you do not refuse him who speaks." (Hebrews 12:25 NIV)** Any other direction we head in is away from God. But obeying His Word keeps us close to Him. This is a type of "dying" that all Christians are expected to do.

REFUSING TO LOOK AT OURSELVES

Furthermore, we can refuse God's leading by refusing to look at what we are really like. Seeing ourselves in God's light absolutely shatters the image of ourselves as loving, kind, basically good people. After getting a small glimpse of what she was really like, one woman told me, "There is black tar inside of me! I'm afraid to look at myself!" Another woman said, "I've been told there is a monster inside of me. I don't want to see it!" One time I watched as an angry, bitter woman spoke. I saw what looked like puffs of soot come out of her mouth! Yet another woman wallowing in self-pity had what looked like a gray veil covering her face, discoloring her whole countenance.

In Christ, we operate in a spiritual realm that is beyond our understanding. These inner giants may seem scary, but their presence can vanish quickly by the delivering power of Christ. The key to their expulsion is to allow God to bring them into full view. Then, with our consent, He will rid us of them.

The Philistine giant Goliath had the whole Israel army frozen in terror by his presence. **"This day I defy the ranks of Israel. Give me a man and let us fight each other." (1 Samuel 17:10 NIV)** No one wanted to be the man to step out and face the giant. I believe there is a whole army of Christians being held at bay simply because they are unwilling to step into the light and face their own ugly, inner giants. How sad to think that the devil can intimidate Christians by using their own emotions against them. If we only realized that a little courage to face the truth, like David's handful of stones, coupled with faith in God could swiftly level those raging inner giants.

REFUSING GOD AS HE IS

Not only are we afraid to face who we are, but we afraid to face who God really is. The immense reality of God frightens us because He overwhelms and consumes us! At Mt. Sinai the Israelites trembled at the sights and sounds of God's presence on the mountain. **"From heaven he made you hear his voice to discipline you. On earth he showed you his great fire while you heard his world coming out of the fire." (Deuteronomy 4:36 NIV)** Later, they pleaded with Moses not to let them experience God that way again. They begged him, **"But now, why should we die? This great fire will consume us, and we will die if we hear the voice of the Lord any longer." (Deuteronomy 5:25 NIV)** Self is shaken to the core at the revealed presence of God. Out of self-preservation, we may avoid getting too close.

There is also an aspect of God's nature which is fiery! Before God commissioned the prophet Isaiah to speak His word, during a vision God cleansed the unclean lips of this man with a burning hot coal. Just as heat sterilizes an instrument, so God's fiery nature must first sterilize those He intends to use to do His holy work. Unfortunately, the fiery nature of God is played way down in the Church. God may be a consuming fire, but we prefer to be cozily warmed.

God sent His final Prophet, Jesus Christ, not to soften the blow against sin and self, but to make God more approachable and understandable. Jesus promised that **"Everyone will be salted with fire."** **(Mark 9:49 NIV)** This meant that God would continue to reveal His fiery nature to deal with our sin. A healthy fear of God should cause us to want Him for His majesty and power. As the cross puts self to death, the holiness of God then becomes our living reality.

∽ Chapter 18 ∽
CIRCUMCISION OF THE HEART

We circumvent the cross mainly because we dread the pain involved. Instinctively, we know that there is no anesthetic for emotional pain. Consequently, we may avoid facing highly-charged personal issues.

For example, a friend of mine volunteered to lead a topical Bible study dealing with the relationship between fathers and daughters. At the onset, group members agreed that they needed to take a close, honest look at how their fathers had impacted them. A couple of months into the study several women quit, while others breezed through the material, denying it had any affect on them. Each week the leader had an increasingly difficult time keeping group members from veering off onto tangents. Even my friend admitted that the subject had been hard for her because she had to re-live so many painful memories. But afterward, she was glad she had finished the study because she felt she had been set free.

There is a deep, deep work of the Holy Spirit that is meant to, at first, wound us, but later free us. This work is called "circumcision of the heart." It is God duplicating the work of crucifixion in our inner being. This is the method God uses on the individual Christian to put self to death. We look to Jesus' crucifixion to understand what God is doing so that we will stick with God through the pain.

God's purpose in this is to sever the constricting ways of sin and self. By slaying the unspiritual parts of us, the Spirit of Christ is unhindered as the controlling power in us. God must get us out of the way so that the Son can come forth through us. **"In him you were also circumcised in the putting of the sinful nature, not with a circumcision done by the hands of man but with the circumcision done by Christ." (Colossians 2:11 NIV)** The Apostle Paul compares this inner work done by God to the cutting of flesh so that we will understand the reason for the pain.

A story in the paper told of a young mother who balked at this procedure for her son. Here is her description of her experience in the hospital: "While my newborn son and daughter were in the neonatal intensive care unit, I witnessed the circumcision of a baby boy…the doctor approached with a sharp instrument. She pulled away the loose skin…and quickly cut it off without giving him anesthesia first… The baby screamed so hard I thought he'd lose his breath. I couldn't watch."[34]

There is no denying our encounter with pain when we go through this inner procedure. By His presence, The Holy Spirit approaches us with His sanctifying intentions. The sharp instrument is the sword of the Spirit, the Word of God which is **"…living and active. Sharper than any double-edged sword, it penetrates even to dividing soul and spirit, joints and marrow; it judges the thoughts and attitudes of the heart." (Hebrews 4:12 NIV)** The glint of the knife is pure truth as it flashes in our hearts, exposing to our recognition our hidden ways. The careful Surgeon must separate the soul from the spirit by cutting off the unredeemed parts of us. Otherwise, our ways, how we are accustomed to thinking and behaving, our human sympathies and strong opinions, will overwhelm our spiritual life in Christ. This spiritual surgery will injure us in our most private parts and slow us down in our activities until we recover.

GOD'S COVENANT

The Father is not squeamish about this operation performed in the hearts of his children. He wants to see Christ emerge from our lives. The fulfillment of our earthly purpose depends on the expres-

---

34   *The Plain Dealer,* Aug. 8, 1995

sion of Christ through us, so it is critical that the old self not get in the way.

It was God's intention to express Himself through people when He entered into an agreement with Abraham. God wanted a people to reflect Himself. The men were to bear the distinct mark of circumcision as a physical sign of the covenant God made with them. **"My covenant in your flesh is to be an everlasting covenant." (Genesis 17:13 NIV)** The result of keeping the covenant would be: 1) God's people would walk blamelessly before Him reflecting God's holiness, 2) His people would be fruitful and multiply, reflecting His limitless creative power and, 3) His people would possess the Promised Land, a picture of provision of eternal life. Ideally, foreign nations would be jealous of Israel and want its God for themselves.

God's goal through Christ is the same on the individual level. Paul makes the application to the inner man. **"A man is not a Jew if he is only one outwardly, nor is circumcision merely outward and physical. No, a man is a Jew if he is one inwardly; and circumcision is circumcision of the heart by the Spirit, not by written code." (Romans 2:29 NIV)** The objectives of the new covenant are the same as originally set: 1) That Christians would live a life of purity before God, 2) That they would become spiritually fruitful and productive and, 3) That they would live out God's purpose in light of eternity. As God expresses Christ through His people, an unbelieving world will see and want Christ also. Repentance is crucially important if we are to be useful under the new covenant.

FREEDOM IN CHRIST

We cannot be useful unless we are first made free. Many Christians are held back from serving God or attending Bible classes or fellowships because of inner turmoil and legal ground which the enemy uses against them. Instead of participating in the Christian body, they stay home.

The Spirit will work to free us from those things which hold us back because, **"It is for freedom that Christ made us free." (Galatians 5:1 NIV)** God will purposely remove hindrances from the

Christian's life to make him free to participate in God's will. As the Holy Spirit removes the unclean, unusable parts of us, we will sense a noticeable lightness and ease in our manner. Let's look at some of the freedoms which are ours in Christ.

Freedom From Our Past

One of the most important areas for us to gain freedom is freedom from our past. Damage that we have suffered from, say a difficult childhood, divorce, or loss of a loved one, can stop us from going on if we do not let the Holy Spirit help us get over our past. Paul voices his own victory by saying, **"I consider everything a loss compared to the surpassing knowledge of knowing Christ Jesus my Lord…But one thing I do, I press on towards the goal to win the prize for which God called me…" (Philippians 3:7-14 NIV)** Paul put all of his life experiences behind him and kept going to be useful for Christ.

Dwelling on the past uses up our time and emotional energy for no good purpose. We cannot keep the past alive in our minds with the false hope of somehow changing it. The past must take its proper place as something over and done. We must ask God to help us let go so that our past will not consume our present and ruin our future. We may never fully understand why life made the turns that it did, but strengthened by Christ, we can face the reality of what happened back when and then move on.

Freedom From Created Things

Another freedom we can have is the freedom from created things. Living in a physical world, we are tempted to put our trust in possessions. The more we own, the more secure we feel. We can also put a high value on something because it seems to represent happiness to us. We think we can't live without it. For instance, I knew a man whose whole identity was wrapped up in his boat. All year he longed for boating season. He used such endearing terms when he talked about it that it seemed to have a human personality! Our idols hold us captive by our desire for them.

God wants our desires to transcend the physical. **"Since then, you have been raised with Christ, set your hearts on things above, where Christ is seated at the right hand of God. Set your minds on things above, not on earthly things." (Colossians 3:11 NIV)** We need to become unfastened from the love of the material so that we can be free to be fascinated with the eternal.

Emotional Freedom

Due to the ministry of the Holy Spirit, we can also have emotional freedom. Christ can settle difficult issues that upset us. He has the power to restrain us from angry moods and reactions; we don't have to be swayed by our strong feelings.

In Scripture, Peter's impulsive emotional responses often got in the way of Christ. **"Peter took him** (Jesus) **aside and began to rebuke him. 'Never Lord', he said, 'This shall never happen to you.' Jesus turned and said to Peter 'Out of my sight, Satan! You are a stumbling block to me...'" (Matthew 16:22-23 NIV)** Peter's overly protective human sympathies and strong heroics were based on powerful feelings within himself. His effort to emotionally extend himself was a potential block to God's will. That is why Jesus rebuked him so strongly. In the same way, our unruly emotions have the potential of pulling us out of God's will.

But cooperation with Christ will bring healing and restoration to our emotions. This is tedious work because we have to learn what feelings are self-based. We can discover emotional freedom as the Spirit works to produce in us the fruit of the Spirit which is: **"love, joy, peace, patience, kindness, goodness, faithfulness, gentleness and self-control." (Galatians 5:22-23 NIV)** The Bible says that there is no law against such things, meaning we are free to become all of these. God won't stop us if we explore our emotional freedom in these ways.

Free To Be Ourselves

As we are cut loose from our past, our possessions, and our pent-up emotions, we can step out with a new boldness and confidence to be ourselves. When our personalities are not loaded down with lies, quirks, and sinful behavior, we can dare to be truthful to the point of transparency.

There is an expression in the world that says, "Fake it 'till you make it!" In other words, make believe you are someone you are not until you become what you think you want to be! Unfortunately, years can be spent in compromise while faking it with no real guarantee of ever making it.

In Christ, we have already made it! There is nothing better we can attain. We must learn to make the most out of the one life God has given us. We don't have to waste time living as phonies. Pretense is foolish because it places importance on a mere facade. If we want to have what is really important and meaningful, then **"... the reality, however, is found in Christ." (Colossians 2:17 NIV)** This means that true, vibrant living is found in Christ and we can live freely in His reality.

THE NOTARY SEAL

Our freedom to be authentic in a lying, faking world is the outward sign of the inner work of circumcision that we bear. God gave me a picture of His work in a believer's life through the description of the notary seal.

The notary seal is an instrument that embosses an original document, attesting to its authenticity. It transforms an ordinary piece of paper into a letter that is respected for its true contents. As the Notary bears down on the seal, the strength of his arm is channeled by the lever onto the place where the seal grips the paper. If too much pressure is applied, then the edge of the seal will totally perforate and tear the document. But if the Notary bears down too little, no one will be able to detect the mark of the seal. After applying the right amount of pressure, the seal is removed, producing a permanent emblem representing the government of that state.

With circumcision of the heart, God wants to "notarize" our hearts so that we would be recognizably His by our character. **"He**

anointed us, set his seal of ownership on us, and put his Spirit in our hearts." (2 Corinthians 1:21 NIV) We are His documentation and our transformation proves God's reality. People read us and know that God exists and that He has personally touched us. And to His glory, before a watching world, we can become the real people in Christ that perhaps we only dreamed we could be.

~ Chapter 19 ~
THE CROSS

Humanity has been cruelly bitten by the Serpent. The poison of sin has infected every man, woman, and child who has ever lived. We find healing and restoration from our crippling condition only as we look to the cross. The cross was the eternal remedy for the poison of sin. As we repent of our sin, the cross provides the power for us to be healed.

The cross was pictured when Israel rebelled against God and then suffered the judgment of poisonous snakes loosed in the camp. The people realized their sin and cried out to Moses. Moses prayed for them and the Lord provided the antidote. **"'Make a snake and put it on a pole; anyone who is bitten can look at it and live.' So Moses made a bronze snake and put it up on a pole. Then when anyone was bitten by a snake and looked at the bronze snake, he lived.'" (Numbers 21 8-9 NIV)** The bronze snake was a prophetic picture of the eventual death of Jesus Christ on the cross. Those who look to His sacrificial death on their behalf will have life eternal.

THE PROVISION OF THE CROSS

As Jesus' body was suspended between Heaven and earth, it was from the cross that God solved the problem of man's sin condition. The provision to set us free was made. The nature of the Serpent was crucified through the human body of Jesus. In one perfect work, the wrath of God was satisfied against sin, the power of sin over humanity was broken, and the way to God was opened for man. **"The Lord will lay bare his holy arm in the sight of all the nations and all the ends of the earth will see the salvation of our God." (Isaiah 52:10 NIV)**

Simple belief in Christ's death as the remedy for our own personal sin is the key to God's pardon and healing. The super-natural event of the cross stands alone as the complete cure for the "snake-bite" of sin universally and individually. We need to be impressed with the magnitude of that day of salvation. God foretold through the prophets that, **"In one day I will destroy sin." (Zechariah 3:8 NIV)** For the vice-like grip of sin to be broken on behalf of the whole world in one day is utterly amazing, yet we must believe it.

I attempted to illustrate the unsurpassing work of the cross to a Sunday school class one morning during Christmas. I had gone to the library and looked up the populations of many countries at different times of civilization. In class we noted thousands of years of human history from all over the globe. Our census quickly filled the chalkboard and went beyond the capabilities of our hand-held calculator.

Then, from my miniature manger scene, I brought out the gold-painted figure of the baby Jesus, the size of a thumbnail. Holding up the tiny shape against the backdrop of numbers which represented a mere glimpse of all humanity, I repeated over and over until my point sunk in, "HE IS ABLE!"

The provision of the cross was made for every human life that ever existed and was sufficient to destroy sin.

THE POWER OF THE CROSS

The supernatural work of Christ was not hindered by numbers, time, degree, nor amount of sin. Man's overwhelming need did not supersede God's saving work. **"Because you were slain, and with your blood you purchased men for God from every tribe and language and people and nation." (Revelation 5:9 NIV)** That the Son of God would take on human flesh, allow His one earthly life to be taken, and his blood spilled as the perfect atoning sacrifice for sin, made the inhabitants of Heaven gasp. Because this provision transcends the ages, the spiritual effects of the cross can be felt in our lives today. We can be significantly changed because of an event that happened almost 2,000 years ago. This fact should make us gasp!

Due to the cross, God is able to penetrate our lives with power in an amount we can stand: **"his incomparably great power for us who believe." (Ephesians 1:19 NIV)** This was the same power that God used to heal me of my depression. His saving power delivered me from my sin and went on to heal my present emotional condition. God holds power which He willingly avails to us as we believe in the perfect work of the cross. We look to Him on the basis of that work.

THE FORGIVENESS OF THE CROSS

From the cross, Christ asked for the forgiveness of the sins of humanity with His dying breath. One of the greatest evidences of the power of the cross is in the felt relief from receiving the Father's forgiveness. When we confess sin and receive God's pardon, a burden is lifted from us and we know it! There is so much power released through forgiveness that the course of people's lives can be changed for good. Where sin had brought death to people, God's forgiveness issues new life. **"And when Jesus had cried out again in a loud voice, he gave us his spirit. At that moment the curtain of the temple was torn in two from top to bottom. The earth shook and the rocks split. The tombs broke open and the bodies of many holy people who had died were raised to life." (Matthew 27:50-52 NIV)**

This same power enables us, who normally hold grudges, to likewise forgive. This most excellent provision of the cross is something we all need to take advantage of for our own good. I'll never forget how wonderful it felt to be free of the hatred I held against my high school boyfriend. As a Christian, I was able to willingly forgive him for how he had hurt me. Those hard feelings of wishing him dead I had carried for years were gone! Like a dead person raised from my tomb, I was set free to go on with my life. The power of the cross is truly evident in the forgiveness of the cross.

THE OFFENSE OF THE CROSS

One would think that people would jump at the chance to take advantage of this wonderful spiritual provision. But grievously, we don't. Why? Because to take advantage of the power of the cross means that we first must admit to ourselves and to God all the wrong we have done.

This magnificent opportunity for healing and deliverance also stands as man's ultimate offense to self. Openly admitting how we were wrong goes against the natural grain of every self-defense reasoning we have. The cross strikes a fatal blow to human pride because it tells us what liars we have been. Our false image of self as being a nice person quickly disintegrates. Christ hung in the spotlight of human history at the cross. But for us to join Him there means stark exposure of everything we've ever done and we abhor seeing that.

We would opt to remove the offense by down-playing sin rather than review and renounce it. "It's not that bad" we tell ourselves. We let ourselves off the hook so casually and easily. By refusing to examine its depths, we can relax and be more at ease with our sin.

But Paul writes, **"In that case the offense of the cross has been abolished." (Galatians 5:11 NIV)** To remove the offense of the cross by down-playing sin neutralizes the effectiveness of its power. We cannot be transformed without the offense of the cross thoroughly intact. To be crucified is to be cured.

OUR PARTICIPATION IN THE CROSS

We will only enjoy this valuable provision and miraculous power by our willing participation in the cross. We must actively seek God to reveal our condition in His light. Otherwise, by human standards, we accept our ways as being normal. For instance, one day on my lunch hour I walked through a city park. I saw a street person pushing a huge cart loaded with garbage. He had everything on it carefully secured: magazines, rags, plastic bottles, newspapers, you name it.

168

I went up to him and asked him if he knew Jesus. He said he had heard of Him but that he couldn't believe in something he couldn't see. I explained to him that sin was the cause of all our troubles. He stared at me blankly. He didn't know what trouble I was talking about. A life aimlessly pushing that cart was normal for him. Although the cart was cumbersome, he trusted in the garbage because it was something he could see and control. If he didn't realize he had a problem, then he wouldn't see his need for a personal Savior, so I left.

We are much like that man hauling that cart. Our sin is a restrictive, yet neatly secured load of garbage within us. Our souls' lover, Jesus Christ, sees our condition and wants to break those inner ties, working to disassemble every filthy piece. His work in us depends on our willingness to see the trouble we are in and not accept the garbage as being normal.

For sinners, like me, who know their need of a personal Savior, the cross becomes a supernatural place of exchange. We can't physically see it or control it, but by faith we can experience it. There, we take off death and put on life, depravity for righteousness, bondage for freedom. We exchange our self-oriented view for God's Christ-centered perspective. Our motives are cleansed as we learn to love in response to the love we have been shown. We exchange falsehood which holds us in darkness for the truth that liberates us to walk in the light.

In another sense, we get undressed before God when we participate in the cross. **"Now Joshua was dressed in filthy clothes as he stood before the angel. The angel said to those who were standing before him, 'Take off his filthy clothes.' Then he said to Joshua, 'See I have taken away your sin, and I will put rich garments on you.'" (Zechariah 3:3-4 NIV)** What we "wear" refers to the way we live. At the cross, we are stripped of our proud, self-sufficient human ways. The old self-seeking life, like a well-worn garment, is removed from us. At the cross, self loses its power to rule as Christ gains access to live through us. Our spiritual life in Christ is the rich garment we wear.

ELIZA DOOLITTLE

I think of another street person portrayed as "Eliza Doolittle" in the film classic *My Fair Lady*. In contrast, she was one who was acutely aware of her hobo status. As she sat in the gutter singing "Wouldn't It Be Loverly?" she dreamed of having a better life. Then she met a voice teacher named Higgins. She decided to abandon all pride and risk looking foolish by showing up on Professor Henry Higgins' doorstep for voice lessons. She told him she wanted to be a lady. The impossibility of her present condition made the challenge even more delightful for Higgins and his friend. The bet was on!

Drill after drill, test after test, Eliza went without food or sleep to accomplish her dream. Her teachers mocked and scorned her as she underwent their discipline. As she came to the end of herself, one morning there was an unexpected breakthrough. The lessons finally stuck and she began speaking like a lady.

Her final test, though, came as she prepared to go to the formal ball to mix company with royalty. That night as she descended the staircase, Higgins stood spellbound at the sight of the glowing creature he had worked to produce. She regally wore a white jeweled gown, diamonds at her neck, and a dazzling crown on her head.

Higgins coaxed her come on but she remained in place at the bottom of the stairs. A real lady does not step out on her own, but waits to be lead by her escort, a sign of proper upbringing. She had learned her lessons well. Her discipline was evident through her behavior.

I re-tell this story because God showed me that it describes the Lady of Scripture—the Church of Jesus Christ. Her Professor is the Holy Spirit who works to train her in the ways of Christ's royalty, making her ready to receive glory and splendor at the end of the age. But she must undergo the discipline of dying in order to be able to carry the glory. She must be a fit vessel for the holy power that will emanate from her.

This also pictures the individual Christian who is willing to look to God and believe for the transformed life. **"They will walk with me, dressed in white, for they are worthy. He who overcomes** will, like them, be dressed in white. I will never erase his name from the book of life, but will acknowledge his name before my father and his angels." (Revelation 3:3-4 NIV) The sparkling white gown is the wardrobe of righteous living before God. We wear the supremacy of Christ like a crown upon our heads as He rules our minds and hearts with sovereignty. We are made worthy only by becoming like Christ.

TRUE CORONATION

One night during a time of prayer, God celebrated my healing and repentance by announcing a new name over me. I saw something like a sparkling crown placed upon my head and heard the voice of God calling me "Disciplined Daughter!" The new name signified the change in my nature. The Father was rejoicing at the transformation that had taken place in me.

Today I glow from having a wonderfully right relationship with my heavenly Father. I have spent years in cooperation with Him to remove the sin barriers that have kept Him at a distance. Now we are close, just as both of us want to be. Our love is mutual and Christ is truly supreme for me.

So when a man at work greets me with, "Good morning, Smiley!" as if I am his ray of hope for the day, I reflect on my hard-won happiness. **"Happy are those whose transgression is forgiven, whose sin is covered. Happy are those to whom their God imputes not iniquity, and in whose spirit is no deceit." (Psalm 32:1-2 NRSV)** I have gone deep to look at sin and self as God saw it in me. The process of dying was painful, but purifying. Now with a cleansed heart, God has made me happy and useful as I joyously submit to the supremacy of Christ. His power is working daily in me. As a result, my life tells the story of how, from Jezebel to Jesus, God is at work through personal repentance transforming the Queen and I have been transformed by the King.

EPILOGUE

Years later I had encounters with both Charlene and the office manager that I mentioned in earlier chapters of this book. In both situations, God was glorified by my Christlike attitudes towards them.

In the case of Charlene, she came to work at the same company that I was now working for. I had made career moves with two companies and was well established at this job when she was hired in as a sales representative. She had changed quite a bit from her provocative demeanor that she brandished when I first met her. We reacquainted ourselves in a cordial way with no friction between us.

One day I was on the phone with her as she called in to ask a question from the field. We chit-chatted a little and I was able to tell her that I was praying for her.

"Yes, Diane, please pray for me! Thank you!"

I was glad to be able to talk to her and treat her well because I genuinely wanted the best for her.

As for the office manager, as I had mentioned, our family was friends with her family. I went with my mother to the funeral service of her mother. I was polite and spoke tenderly to her as I offered my condolences. She was divorced by now and living in another city.

The pastor gave a noteworthy sermon celebrating the honorable life of her Christian mother. As they closed the casket, the office manager stood by herself away from other family members and cried. I went over to her and held her as she crumbled in my arms sobbing. Afterwards, I gave her my phone number and said she could call me if she ever needed prayer.

In both these situations, it is evident that it is not God's will for people to be banished from His presence, no matter how much mis-guided living they have done. God even gives Jezebel time and opportunities to repent.

Now that you have read this material, you may realize your own need to repent before God. The Bible says, **"Repent, then, and turn to God, so that your sins may be wiped out..." (Acts 3:19)** By doing so, you can know Jesus Christ personally and experience His life-changing power for yourself. He is only a prayer away. You can believe in Him and meet Him with these words.

"DEAR JESUS,

I BELIEVE THAT YOU ARE THE SON OF GOD. I BELIEVE THAT YOU CAME TO EARTH AND DIED ON A CROSS TO PAY FOR THE SINS OF THE WHOLE WORLD. I BELIEVE YOU WERE RAISED FROM THE DEAD AND YOU ARE NOW SEATED IN HEAVEN.

I ADMIT THAT I AM A SINNER BEFORE YOU AND I AM WILLING TO CHANGE. I WANT TO TURN AWAY FROM MY SIN AND TURN TO YOU. I AM SORRY, PLEASE FORGIVE ME.

NOW, JESUS, I ASK YOU TO COME INTO MY LIFE AND TAKE FULL CONTROL. PLEASE SHOW ME HOW TO LIVE A LIFE THAT IS PLEASING TO GOD. THANK YOU. AMEN"

If you sincerely meant that prayer, you can be sure that Christ has entered your life by faith in Him. The Bible says, **"I write these things to you who believe in the name of the Son of God so that you may know that you have eternal life." (1 John 5:13)** God bless you as you follow and serve the Lord Jesus Christ!

REFERENCES

Anderson, Neil T., *Helping Others Find Freedom In Christ,*
Regal Books, Ventura, 1995

Bakker, Jim, *I Was Wrong,* Thomas Nelson Publishers,
Nashville, 1996

Chambers, Oswald, *My Utmost For His Highest*, Barbour and
Company, Westwood, 1935

"The Cleveland Plain Dealer", Plain Dealer Publishing Co.,
Cleveland, OH

Ernst, Carl H. & Zug, George R., *Snakes In Question,* Smithsonian
Institution Press, Washington D.C., 1996

Graham, Billy, *The Holy Spirit,* Word Publishing, Dallas, 1978

Joyner, Rick, *Epic Battles Of the Last Days*, MorningStar
Publications, Charlotte, 1986

Joyner, Rick, *There Were Two Trees In The Garden*, MorningStar
Publications, Charlotte, 1995

Kassian, Mary A., *The Feminist Gospel*, Crossway Books,
Wheaton, 1992

Mains, David, *Thy Kingship Come*, Zondervan Publishing House, Grand Rapids, 1989

Meyer, Joyce, *Beauty For Ashes*, Harrison House, Inc., Tulsa, 1994

Minirth, Frank, M.D. & Meier, Paul, M.D., *Happiness Is A Choice* Baker Books, Grand Rapids, 1978

Murphy, Dr. Ed, *The Handbook Of Spiritual Warfare*, Thomas Nelson Publishers, Tennessee, 1992

Murray, Andrew, *Humility*, Whitaker House, Springdale, 1982

North, Gary, *Unholy Spirits*, Dominion Press, Ft. Worth, 1988

Peale, Norman Vincent, *The Power Of Positive Thinking*, Prentice-Hall, Inc., 1952

Pride, Mary, *The Way Home*, Crossway Books, Wheaton, 1985

Playfair, William L., M.D., *The Useful Lie*, Crossway Books, Wheaton, 1991

Reed, John W., *1100 Illustrations From The Writings Of D.L. Moody*, Baker House Books, Grand Rapids, 1996

Scott, Catherine L., *Breaking The Cycle Of Abuse*, David C. Cook Publishing Co., Elgin, 1988

Silvious, Jan, *Please Don't Say You Need Me*, Pyranee Books, Grand Rapids, 1989

Smalley, Gary & Trent, John, Ph.D., *The Blessing*, Thomas Nelson Publishers, Nashville, 1979

Streisand, The Pictorial Biography, Courage Books,
        Philadelphia, 1997

"Time Magazine", Time, Inc. New York, 1998

"The Wall Street Journal", Wall Street Publishing, New York, 1996

Vanderbilt, Arthur T., II, *Fortune's Children, The Fall Of The
        House Of Vanderbilt,* William Morrow and Company, Inc.,
        New York, 1989

Wiersbe, Warren W., *Why Us? When Bad Things Happen To
        God's People,* Baker Book House Co., Grand Rapids, 1984

Wright, H. Norman, *Always Daddy's Girl,* Regal Books,
        Ventura, 1989

Made in the USA
Charleston, SC
21 January 2012